Dreams in Which I'm Almost Human

Dreams IN WHICH I'm Almost Human

a memoir

HANNAH SOYER

Red Hen Press | *Pasadena, CA*

Dreams in Which I'm Almost Human

Book layout by Ava Morgan

CIP Data has been applied for with the Library of Congress
ISBN-13 (tradepaper): 978-1-63628-474-3
ISBN (eBook): 978-1-63628-475-0
ISBN (Library edition): 978-1-63628-484-2

The National Endowment for the Arts, the Los Angeles County Arts Commission, the Ahmanson Foundation, the Dwight Stuart Youth Fund, the Max Factor Family Foundation, the Pasadena Tournament of Roses Foundation, the Pasadena Arts & Culture Commission and the City of Pasadena Cultural Affairs Division, the City of Los Angeles Department of Cultural Affairs, the Audrey & Sydney Irmas Charitable Foundation, the Meta & George Rosenberg Foundation, the Albert and Elaine Borchard Foundation, the Adams Family Foundation, Amazon Literary Partnership, the Sam Francis Foundation, and the Mara W. Breech Foundation partially support Red Hen Press.

First Edition
Published by Red Hen Press
www.redhen.org

For those who came before me and those who will come after.

And for my family, blood-related and not.

The following text contains discussions of abuse, ableism, medical trauma, death, self-harm, and suicidal ideation. Please take care while reading.

(It also features cats, mermaids, plants, sunsets, laughter, poetry, and music.)

The body is not bounded by the skin, where we understand the skin to be a kind of container for the self, but rather our bodies always extend and connect to other bodies . . . and to practices, techniques, technologies and objects which produce different kinds of bodies and, arguably, different ways of enacting what it means to be human and non-human.

—Lisa Blackman, "Embodying Affect"

I don't believe it, though at the same time, like so many other miracles
having to do with the merfolk, I don't not *believe it.*
It seems there might be a factual basis for the story,
which is more than can be said of some of the other yarns they spin.

—Nuala Ní Dhomhnaill, "Bunmhiotas na Murúch/Founding Myth" from *The Fifty Minute Mermaid,* translated by Paul Muldoon

Dreams in Which
I'm Almost Human

Preface

In the beginning, a mermaid fell from the stars into the body of the ocean, glitter of light splashed onto water.

Because she came from the sky, her body was ill-adapted for the sea. The mermaids who made their home in the ocean looked at her and saw something familiar (themselves), but also something foreign. The stardust void that turned their stomachs. They wanted to both protect and leave this mermaid in equal measures.

Special gills were surgically added to the mermaid's neck so she could better breathe. Some wondered what a mermaid was doing in the sky to begin with, but an answer was never given, never known. The stories they sang about her filled her ears each night as she pulled her new body through water, closing her eyes to the glint of a knife in bright relief against the backs of her eyelids. Sometimes the words became her muscles and sinew, replacing the blood in her veins with sentences not her own. She didn't know what to become.

Sometimes the world loved the mermaid. Sometimes it didn't. Sometimes it opened up doors in front of her through which she could disappear, enticing her with a whispered *You never belonged here, you know. Look at all the reasons why.* She never stepped through these doors (yes, stepped). When the doors tempted her, she made herself think, instead, of the way sunlight touched the leaves of the ivy that grew along the coast—she was certain that this wouldn't happen on the other side of the doors. She wasn't willing to give such a sight up.

On certain nights, she'd dream of other sky-mermaids and the worlds they inhabited. Each night the storyline changed, except for the glass her dream-hands pressed against. Sometimes, the boundary shattered, and she swam through into this new world. This was the mermaid's strength.

Do you want to know the mermaid's weakness? She fell too hard and too quickly for those who walked upright on two legs. A sailor once spotted her (at this point she wasn't trying to hide from them) and told her (forgive him) that she was too beautiful for this world. The mermaid spent a year trailing his boat, trying to put words to the feeling inside her, trading out one word for another until she saw his arm slung around a human girl and landed (with a sick sort-of certainty) on *pain*.

She fell next for a writer girl, her words slamming into her heart and cracking her open. Then an artist with long hair that caught the moonlight, and another girl who kissed softly and sweetly. A girl who wrote poems for the mermaid, coaxing out confessions, and then a girl who broke her.

After each burst of connection and subsequent combustion, the mermaid would unspool what had happened in her hands, trying to make sense of where a narrative stuttered and failed. Was it her sky origins that caused a coming together to fall apart? The slice of her gills? The way she vowed each night to survive? She doesn't know. She doesn't know, either, if a reason matters.

I know your instinct will be to read this fish-woman as me. I'm asking you to forsake the metaphor.

This is a Truth

I can't stumble into a room, but it would be disingenuous to describe the sensation any other way. This is how words have carved out little spaces of meaning in our collective minds.

When I arrive in Iowa City, I'm living on my own for the first time, at college, 120 miles away from home, and I'm running on four years of pent-up anger at my friend Caroline's death. Little flickers of heat that would rupture my skin and leave me stumbling in an alley after one too many yeses (if I could stumble), or feet pounding the pavement beneath me during midnight excursions across the bridge spanning the Iowa River (if my feet ever touched the ground), or hands shoving someone back, someone off, someone away (if my arms had the strength to push a body).

The meanings of words change. Categories are unstable. The writer is not the narrator and the narrator is not the writer; that sort of thing. I still don't know what words can be proof of— a death? A life? A love?

See—

No Other Choice

This story begins with a river, forceful and true.

There was the time my dad's brothers and sisters put the youngest of them in a basket and let it float down the Middle Raccoon River in their hometown of Carroll, Iowa. The girls were playing at being Miriam, hiding bundles of life in woven wicker containers and sending it away, away, away. The boys were just being boys.

I've been to Carroll a handful of times, years and years and years ago. I can't picture the Raccoon River realistically, but of course my mind has created its own images of this space and life––the rolling green of the farm where my dad lived for four years before moving to another house in the town, the Catholic high school he attended (or semi-attended, days in the classroom traded for alcohol after the loss of his mom), and, of course, the winding river.

I'm trying to write a story about a small town in Iowa and the ghosts it holds, and so I search through old Carroll newspapers for mention of my last name. *Soyer* shows up in the scanned pages of the *Carroll Daily Times Herald* from April 20, 1936, twenty-two years before my dad was born. You could say the headlines form their own little poem, hold their own veiled meanings:

> *Frank Stork of Breda Dies Here Sunday.* Frank Stork had eleven children, so I guess that makes it worth it. *Funeral Rites Wednesday for Carroll Woman.* Carroll Woman doesn't get a name in the headline, like Frank

> Stork does. *One of Trio Trapped in Mine Succumbs; Expect to Reach Others Today.* You had to be resilient to survive then and there. More than that, though, you needed the ability to outsmart death. Except that's impossible. Isn't it?

One day my dad climbed into a car and, with his chubby child hands, somehow took it out of park. It went rolling into the ditch, but he wasn't injured. His mom died from an aneurysm when he was nine. His older sister Kathy dropped out of the convent where she was learning to be a bride of Jesus and came back home to raise the kids. There were ten of them—until my dad's dad remarried and had another kid plus two stepchildren, and then there were thirteen. Carroll Woman, identified by the 1936 article only as Mrs. Henry Soyer, didn't even get a name in the newspaper. My grandma Maizie Soyer will.

My dad had his first drink at twelve, three years after his mom died. He took a year off from college to work on a fishing boat for his Uncle Charlie off the coast of California at twenty-two. My dad's body did not agree with the ocean. He got terribly seasick each time they would go out to sea, so seasick, in fact, the other workers on the boat had to tie him to the boom. They fished cod and sole, and sometimes salmon got caught in their nets unawares. Thirty-eight years later, my parents took a trip up the coast, stopping at various towns my dad was familiar with, including Fort Bragg, where he had left port from. Later, my mom told me that they hadn't stayed long in this town, that the past lives and past selves flitting around this town meant my dad had been itching to leave.

My history, at least what's important for this story, is this: I was eight years old when my body was cut open by a room of white-coated, blank-faced men. They did this, fused a titanium rod to my spine, in order to save my life. Without it, my lungs would have eventually collapsed because the muscles surrounding them would grow too weak to support them. I did not consent to this, nor did I have to. The summer after I graduate from my undergrad at the University of Iowa while doing research for my application to grad school, I come across a statistic that makes the green grass of the park I am in blur and warp between my eyes: 20 percent of people who undergo spinal fusion surgery are later (formally) diagnosed with PTSD. I don't know if this label applies to me. If it does, I don't know what it means. The scary thing about words is that once you are given those to describe what happened to you, you can make an event from your past more real. Real is probably not the right word—what does *nonfiction* really mean, anyway?

"It was the hardest thing we ever had to do," my mom told me once, in reference to my spinal fusion surgery. Later, this is the exact same phrase I use to describe my first year of grad school: my first year living out of state, my first year fully immersed in a creative space that made it all too clear I'd have to fight like hell to belong there with my othered body and clunky wheelchair, my first year fully extricated from the binds that had tied me to a man I thought I loved, my first year realizing I am primarily attracted to women, my first year getting a drug injected into my spinal fluid that is meant to stop symptoms of my disease and possibly reverse them—a drug valued at $180,000 per injection (I have no understanding of what this number means, only that it makes apparent sense to pharmaceuticals and insurance companies), my first year of grappling with the truth that I am drawn to situations in which I am forced to make difficult choices for the sole reason that in these moments, I actually have a say.

When I got into grad school, I thought I was going to write a book about control, inheritance, and disability. That's what I put in my cover letter: *I'm writing a book about control, inheritance, and disability.* But in the time between applying to programs and then getting accepted, and then sitting in my first workshop and thinking, *Ok, well how will this relate to the book?* a lot can happen, and a lot can change. Take, for example, my growing understanding of the term *manipulation*. Take, for example, the visceral breaking of my heart. Take, for example, the election of a man who bragged about sexually assaulting women to the highest public office in our country, and the fallout from his actions.

On December 23, 2016, about a month and a half after America elected someone through fear, the power of words, and varied definitions of consent, the FDA announced its approval of Spinraza, the first ever treatment drug for Spinal Muscular Atrophy. I felt uncomfortable about this, even more so because I felt guilty for feeling uncomfortable. I wanted to be ecstatic, crying happy tears as so many other people affected by my disease were. But I couldn't help wondering if this approval would contribute to the overall belief that money should not be spent on services to help disabled people live as they are. And with the new presidential administration scheduled to take over in less than a month, under a party that has historically been against expanding the programs such as Medicaid that many disabled people rely on to live, surely this was already in jeopardy.

It was. On June 22, 2017, sixty disability rights activists from national disability rights group ADAPT are arrested and forcibly removed from Senate Majority Leader Mitch McConnell's office after staging a "die-in" as a form of protest to the Better Care Reconciliation Act, a bill spearheaded by Senate Republicans that included large cuts to Medicaid. The name of this bill was purposefully misleading. Die-ins, on the other hand, are exactly what they sound like—protests similar to "sit-ins," where participants occupy an area, usually a governmental building or office, and refuse to leave until their demands are met. Unlike a sit-in, in a die-in, participants do not just occupy a space with their bodies, they pretend to be dead as a symbol of both the past and the potential future—these are the bodies of those who have died from this policy, this war, this disease, and these are the bodies of those who will die if nothing is done. In die-ins, participants are both themselves and others, one and many.

Members of the June 2017 die-in are not just forcibly removed from McConnell's office; some are also forcibly removed from their wheelchairs. Others, who had removed themselves from their wheelchairs to lay on the office and hallway floor, are carried out of the Capitol, their mode of movement, their freedom, their other body left behind.

The threat of insufficient care posed by the Better Care Reconciliation Act and other measures like it isn't just hypothetical—it's a battle I know too well. Most of the time, care covered by Medicaid is not enough, even as-is; the threat of cutting what little care *is* provided is criminal. I don't have examples of other people with my level of needs living the way I want to live. Some are living at home with their parents, others are living in a duplex right next to their parents, and still others are living on their own, relying on unreliable agency services which leave them in bed for hours on end during the day. For the first two options, I'm not sure what happens when their parents are no longer able to take care of them. I really don't know. *Institutionalization* was such a hazy concept to me not too long ago.

When we are faced with stories we can't believe, unbelievable because of their horror, we do what's in the name—we don't believe them. To allow such a story to be true would be admitting our reality and our world is not as it seems. There's danger in this for those on the outside, for those who are not directly impacted by such stories. We all know this: People not faced with the threat of no care, a lack of options, or assault (take your pick) can say, *No, I can't believe something like that would happen, it's simply not possible in this country, this year.* And then they can turn away, letting the image presented to them of how life is for some other people slide away.

But if you are one of these *other people,* how do you acknowledge this reality while not admitting defeat? What I'm trying to say: I don't know if these are the right stories to be telling, or where the exact balance is between laying bare hard truths and allowing them to overtake your every move, giving them enough power to finish your own story. What I'm trying to say: there's no way around what I've inherited from my community—the sharp need for other people and a sharp fear of losing them.

Some adults who choose to pursue Spinraza are able to receive the injection at a point in the spine that has not been fused. Some adults have pockets in between the rod and their spine where the needle can reach the spinal fluid. Some adults have to have a hole drilled in their rod to make space for the needle. This means going under, being cut back open. Not nearly as intensive of a surgery as spinal fusion, which often entails an incision from neck to tailbone and can last anywhere from two to seven hours (my mom remembers mine lasting around three and a half), but a surgery nonetheless.

After the drug received FDA approval, I moved forward with investigating which of these categories I fall into. I didn't know, yet, if I wanted to receive this new treatment, but I did know that I wanted all the facts. I got a CT scan and was emailed the results within a week: *If contemplating intrathecal injection, there is a narrow window posteriorly at L5-S1 with the thecal sac terminating at this level which may not provide adequate access as it is at the far inferior aspect of the thecal sac.* This is a gray area, I realized. In fact, this isn't an answer at all. I have no control over this because I don't know what these words mean.

University of Iowa Hospitals and Clinics eventually tells me they'd have to drill a hole in my spine. Kansas, where I've accepted my position in the MFA program for creative writing, tells me there is an opening between my fusion and my spine, that they can inject me, no problem. There's not one simple answer as to why I said yes.

Months before my childhood spinal fusion surgery, after my whole family gave samples of blood, it was determined that my dad, a type O, would be the one to donate two pints of blood that would eventually be pumped into my body to replace what I lost during my surgery. He couldn't drink coffee for twenty-four hours before they siphoned out his blood, and this left him with a pounding headache. He gave up, briefly, the ability to think in peace, so that my lungs would not be threatened with eventual collapse under my curving spine.

The titanium fused to my spine makes it more difficult for me to receive Spinraza, which has to be injected directly into the spinal fluid. In clinical trials, Spinraza was tested on very young children and adolescents, people who hadn't had spinal fusion surgery. An 18-gauge,

5- to 8-inch needle is placed into the spinal fluid, and after a magic number of injections, *voila*, increased muscle function. Of course, this is a lot more reductive than the actual process, but the key detail is that easy access to the patients' spines was necessary for the clinical trials to even move forward. Adults with my disease, almost all of whom have matching spinal rods inside our bodies, are faced with the same question after the FDA's approval of the new drug: How will the needle get around our rods? How will we reconcile our body's truth that one treatment only ends up getting in the way of another?

Now, every time I go to KU Med Center in Kansas City to have a needle stuck into my side (every four months for maintenance doses), I have to sign a consent form. Am I consenting to the pressure in my hip, the sharpness of the needle brushing past my femoral nerve bundle, the burning of fear that inevitably turns into a panic attack on the operating table and accompanies each $180,000 injection (which, miraculously, is covered by insurance and then the drug company)? I don't know, but I keep signing that form. Medical consent is not the same as sexual consent, but there are ways in which they blend together. The boundaries of bodily autonomy, questions of power, questions of abuse and choice and agency diverge, converge, diverge again.

On May 24, 2019, Avexis is approved by the FDA as a gene therapy drug for children with SMA two years old and younger. Because this drug actually targets and changes the gene that SMA is imprinted on, Avexis is, for all intents and purposes, not a treatment but a cure. It would be easy to reduce this event to either a milestone in a decades-long search for a cure, or the inevitable beginning of an eradication of not just a disease, understand, but a people—my people. The reality is, I think, more complex than either of these easily pinpointed truths. In a few generations, it's likely that there will be no more people with SMA, and with this, the threat of an eventual extinction of our stories. The scar down my back from my spinal fusion surgery is also my favorite part of my body. It is definitive. There is no question as to its existence.

I had a distant cousin who was born with the same disease I have. SMA is genetic, so it makes sense. When Ava is born, I think, *My God, I have SMA ancestors, somewhere. I wish I could have known them.* It's unlikely that any past family members who had SMA would have outlived childhood, but I want to imagine a world in which they did, a world in which we find each other across oceans, across generations—our eyes sparking in a recognition of and ode to our beautifully crumpled bodies. What stories have I inherited from them? A sense of not belonging, of being too much to care for, of an early death or removal to somewhere hidden away, or the enduring truth that we create and adapt and are thus still here?

I met Ava once, at a picnic held for families with children with SMA. She was sitting in her stroller and shy like a one-year-old who had just woken up from a nap. She had that squinty look of skepticism I recognize from photos of myself at that age. When Ava passes away on November 5, 2016, at fifteen months old, two and a half years before Avexis, my mom and aunt go to Carroll for the funeral, and of course, I think of the river. Always changing, but always there, until humans bring about its disappearance.

Things have changed, and they haven't. I'm still writing a book about disability, control, and inheritance.

In early October of my first year of grad school, an hour after Brett Kavanaugh is confirmed as a Supreme Court Justice by the US Senate, I attend a reading of another woman in my program, a reading I think I may have to miss because at this point, all I want to do is curl in on myself on my bedroom floor, something my body is incapable of doing. When my uncle texts me, *How are you doing?* I want to respond with, *I don't want to understand how this happened, but I think I do understand. When are we going to talk about the fact that we don't talk about politics?*

A week or so later, amid all the stories and hurt swirling around Kavanaugh, my mom calls me. "We just got back from sitting out on the patio at Grandma and Grandpa's." My mom's brother—my uncle—was visiting from a suburb of Chicago, where my mom is from. Selected books from the coffee table at my grandparent's house: *Pantsuit Nation*, *Hard Choices*, *Obama: An Intimate Portrait*.

My mom is one of four siblings, two brothers and one sister. All of my cousins on her side are boys, except Sarah, the daughter of my mom's sister. There's a photo of Sarah and me as kids on the couch in our living room. My arms are wrapped protectively around her shoulders, and I'm smiling into the distance. She looks straight at the camera, as if both trying to figure out how it works and daring it to contain her. This is the best description I can give of our relationship—going into the world, armed with each other, until the end. When Sarah starts college, also in Kansas, there's a span of time where she answers each of my *how are you*'s with a tired *living the dream*.

That day, my mom had asked her brother what the other side of his family thought of everything going on. "They love him," he had said, and it didn't even matter what *him* he was referring to. "And your sons?" My mom voices truths I hope to one day have the courage to say aloud. "They're the next generation, you know. They need to be aware of this. They need to be voting." These are three sentences I would not have had the strength to speak. "You're right," my uncle had responded to my mom. "I know, you're right."

When these cousins visit my grandparents, the sounds of laughter mix with the grunts of their fighting, wrestling on the floor, a "Stop, Joe," from the youngest boy, a "stop" that is often ignored. It is my grandma who always has to say, "Boys, knock it off," from her stance in the kitchen—where she is often preparing more food than we need—while my uncle sits in a chair, feet crossed, reading a newspaper. After my grandma intervenes, my uncle will rouse himself, look up from the headlines, and echo his mother's words.

There are many ways to look at the above anecdote, some of them positive: "In many ways, we didn't feel like we could express our anger growing up," my mom will tell me, "and so I think, really, the play-fighting is healthy, something we wouldn't have seen as children." I'm not telling this story in hopes of painting my cousins and uncle as aggressive and complacent—they are, in fact, gentle and fun-loving in turns, taking care of shelter dogs, going skydiving, meeting my friends and me for donuts and hot chocolate in downtown Chicago. To be clear, this isn't even about my uncle. This isn't even about those cousins. Dissecting a single moment into the multitude of factors that builds to an interaction is not what this is about. It is about a pattern of responsibility, and a questioning of who is most often cast in the role of caretaker.

Once, as my mom and I are in the kitchen with her, my mom and grandma getting our veggie burgers ready, my grandma opens the refrigerator door and sticks her head in to look for the hamburger buns. "Well, we only have three. The boys can have them, and we can have bread." My mom and I looked at each other, a *what the hell* in the space where our eyes meet. "Mom, no. Whoever wants a bun can have a bun. And whoever wants bread can have bread."

Sure, yes, it's just bread. It's just the choices we are given of what we want to eat. But in this instance, the *boys* my grandma was referring to were my other uncle who lives with my grandparents, my dad, and my grandpa.

My grandpa's mom was abused by his dad, and my grandma's mom tore down a wall in her house when she got tired of waiting for her husband to do it. My grandma took care of four children and seven grandchildren and now takes care of my grandpa as he gets older, sometimes giving until there's nothing left to give. My mom stayed.

I'm not sure which inheritance has shaped me more—that of the women in my family who came before me, or that of my non-blood community, my Crip siblings and ancestors. I am someone with stories written on my body because of how my body is made, how it looks, how it inhabits the world—I need people to help me in order to live, a need that is painted as beautiful by some and horrible by others. I need care, and I have been raised by women who take care of others.

Somewhere in the long line of mothers that have birthed and raised and carried on a name not even their own, I inherited a "defective" SMN1 gene. If I have kids—which I don't see in my future, but I'll entertain for the purpose of this story—I'll pass this gene on, along with the likelihood of brown hair, high cheekbones, a pinky that curves inward. But, of course, this isn't all I'll be passing on. My grandma is one of the strongest women I know, and my mom speaks in times when I freeze up and keep my mouth shut. Still, there are other truths. Are the cards that I am dealt, made of my foremothers' lives, random, a toss-up? Are they out of my control? Do I even want to know what I've inherited from the women that came before me?

My mom, who left her high school boyfriend because he didn't want her to go to college, who fell in love with my dad and his non-sober ways, who took my older brother and left one night when she got home from work and found the house torn apart as my dad searched for the keys to go buy more beer. My mom and my brother came back, my dad eventually stopped drinking, but that's not the point. She left her job as a graphic designer when I was born.

My grandma, whose dad wrote letters to her from the South Pacific during his time in the Navy, who never went to college and who raised four children and worked at a music store ("it was a way to bring other people joy," she told me) and followed my grandpa, the park ranger, across the country with babies trailing behind her and growing inside of her.

And my other grandma, my dad's mom, who died when he was nine and who loved daisies and who ultimately gave birth to ten children because their family was Catholic and that was her role to play.

Which of these were choices autonomously being made, and which were choices forced upon them? *You have no other choice*—is this a correct use of the word?

Hard Shells

There was the squirrel my mom killed while in Colorado with my dad, before my brother and I were born. She slowed down to let it cross the road and then came a dart and a run and a realization that sometimes we are the hands used to suck life out of other bodies. My mom had to pull over on the mountain pass, stumble out of the car, dry heave into the bushes.

The instinct to curl in on oneself is a desire to protect that part of you that is most vulnerable, and also keeps you alive. In water, I am the same as when I was in my mom's womb, able to move around through water and blood, draw my knees up to my chest, wrap my arms around my legs, another barrier of flesh and bone around the beating muscle sheltered behind my sternum.

The turtles were a cruel trick of nature, their mother having crossed the road of our newly developed neighborhood to lay her eggs in the pond behind the house of a boy I thought one day I might decide to have a crush on, leaving the babies to get flattened by cars on the trek back across the road to their home—shells crushed like the walnuts my brother would smash with his heel whenever we found them on bike trails. We started rescuing them when we saw them, taking them to our backyard where our dad waited with the kiddie pool he had filled with water and minnows he had gotten for food. The first two brought home we named Paint and Pint. Pint was the smaller of the two, and this, mixed with the way my mouth formed his name, made me want to protect him forever.

My friend Caroline's favorite animal was the turtle. *Was* as in past tense. Like so many things, I did not learn this about her until after she died.

As a child, I imagined myself a pharaoh each night in bed, my arms crossed against my chest. King Tut never made it to adulthood, and yet the world wouldn't let him die, evidenced by his shell of a sarcophagus inside his shell of a tomb, preserved in the *National Geographics* my brother and I would page through thousands of years later. As a semi-adult, I would come across this line from disability rights lawyer and writer Harriet McBryde Johnson: "While anyone can die young, it's not something you can count on. You have to be prepared to survive."

There was the day, then, when Pint went missing, and although we searched every inch of our yard, roping in the neighbor kids to help, we never found him. Precarious, searching for a tiny living creature in a kingdom of grasses being flattened by the feet and knees of my brother and our friends, the tires of my wheelchair. Later, my brother sat on the back of our van crying as my dad explained to us both that life is life because of death.

There was the opossum on our way home from my grandparents', angry eyes flashing in the light reflected from our headlights, eyes made mirrors by our machine. It writhed and snarled and frothed in the dark that night afforded it, and to this day I thank the forces that kept me buckled in the middle of the van, unable to crane my neck and look out the window toward the source of the blood, witnessing the half of the opossum's body that had been mangled beyond recognition (was that the tail?), plastered to the cement of the road. My dad said we had to hit the rest of it, that it was mercy, that we couldn't let it stay there, stuck to the road and in pain and not knowing why it couldn't move. My mom put her face in her hands, and I could see the image burned on the back of her eyelids.

I would later have paintings of mermaids hung in my apartment, each woman curled around her tail. A fetus beginning. I still don't know if mermaids bleed. I still don't know if mermaids fuck. The instinct to curl in on oneself is a desire to protect that part of you that is most vulnerable, and also keeps you alive.

There was the grasshopper that flew the wrong way into the path of my brother's bike as we rode up and down, up and down my neighbor's driveway. This evisceration I saw. Wings crushed, insides oozing, legs twitching as the insect tried to free itself from the force binding it to that hot, sun-splattered pavement. My brother pressed down on the brakes, skidded to a halt. *We have to kill it,* he said. I don't remember if we did.

My mom collected arrowheads before she met my dad, carefully formed flint that could pierce through the skin of any intruder, perhaps the most solid thing for her to latch onto during family camping trips with my park ranger grandfather and the woman who walked tall beside him, a woman who embraced her life, her family, the adventure of motherhood. Still, she always wanted more music. This was after my grandpa's brother burned down the family farm. I don't know if my mom's own brother had yet to shave his eyebrows off and hitchhike across the country. I now have an image of an arrowhead tattooed on my breastbone, a mermaid carved into my shoulder. What barriers of flesh and bone did my mom forge around her own heart? What would I learn to forge around my own?

Reasons for the Present

I.

This story begins with drawers. Drawers like boxes, boxes like chests, chests like hollows under the floorboards where secrets are kept. Drawers like those that my mom has told me to put everything into before I go to bed each night, on nights when we are sleeping under the same roof. A letting go of what is too heavy to carry into my dreams.

From *Peter Pan,* a book we have read together countless times—first her reading it to me, then me reading it to her: "Mrs. Darling first heard of Peter when she was tidying up her children's minds. It is the nightly custom of every good mother after her children are asleep to rummage in their minds and put things straight for next morning, repacking into their proper places the many articles that have wandered during the day. If you could keep awake (but of course you can't) you would see your own mother doing this and you would find it very interesting to watch. It's quite like *tidying up drawers.*"

When my brother and I were younger, my mom read to us each night before we went to bed. It's how she taught us to assign everything else to the drawer, how to conjure new stories before closing our eyes.

II.

Sylvia Llewelyn Davies was born into a family of artists and wordsmiths. But what she is remembered for is creating. Her sons, George, Jack, Peter (see: Pan), Michael, and Nicholas, would eventually find themselves characters in a children's book about a boy who never grew up, a book in which daughters and granddaughters and great granddaughters are tasked with taking care of a boy whose refusal to face reality is masked by his charismatic thirst for adventure.

No one knows the extent of Sylvia's relationship to J. M. Barrie, the man who wrote *Peter Pan*. Her husband, Arthur Llewelyn Davies, died when she was forty years old, three years before cancer in her chest killed her. She and Barrie had been close since she met him at a dinner party when she was thirty-two and discovered he was already friends with her sons. He provided emotional and financial support to her and the boys, especially after Arthur's death. Shortly after Sylvia's own death, Barrie told the boys they had been engaged. Her sons doubted this, especially Peter and Jack. In the context of this story, I'm not sure it matters. Someone had to inspire the creation of Wendy Darling, right?

The man I thought I loved once told me that he liked stories, but would rather listen to them being read to him than read them himself. When the first Harry Potter book came out—he was eight—his mother gave it to him to read and he tore through the first pages in frustration, unable to comprehend how all the words on the page came together to create a linear, coherent tale. *I threw it across the room,* he told me, with a low chuckle that turned the pit of my stomach into jelly.

The man I thought I loved was a friend of a friend, the older brother to a boy with another form of Muscular Dystrophy. We met when he asked me to be on the disability advocacy YouTube show he did with my friend, to talk about the US healthcare debacle that was the 2017 Better Care Reconciliation Act. Months later, he messaged me again, and our back and forth became day in and day out, our own unfurling story I held onto with an iron grip.

His voice made my skin sing, and if he wanted to, he could have turned me inside out, licked clean every organ and bone. Because this feeling of terrifying surrender left me stumbling (a metaphor, of course), I offered to read to him, like my mother read to my brother and me: stories stretched thin across phone lines and miles, stories built from a hope that he would stay, stories to keep the darkness of other stories at bay.

One such other story: *I lay in a bathtub once and let the blood drip down my arms,* the man told me. *It was art.* My stomach lurched. Every cell in my body screamed *no.* I knew then that I would drop whatever I was doing if his name lit up my phone screen, that I would stop my own day to stop him from doing that again.

I have language for that, now: *codependency.* But when I experienced it, I just knew it as love plus pain.

III.

Love plus pain are heady ingredients for a story.

In the book version of *Peter Pan,* Wendy's daughter has to carry on the heartbreaking work of taking care of Peter once Wendy has "grown up," and her daughter after that and her daughter after that. At one point, Wendy asks, "How do you think of me, Peter?" and Peter Pan says, "I think of you as an adoring son would." Wendy's entire existence revolves around caretaking, and according to the text, Wendy likes it. I'm not sure that she did.

Wendy is acting out learned behavior. To what extent was—am—I? Mrs. Darling was once the bride of Neverland, also, and keeps Peter's kiss in the very corner of her lips, where her children and husband can never catch it. Although it is written that she first comes across the name Peter one night when she is going through her children's minds (where is the boundary between caretaking and smothering?), we as the reader know this isn't true, that this is merely a way for J. M. Barrie to prolong our realization that Wendy is not the first Darling (and won't be the last) to try to save the Lost Boys.

The book doesn't end this way, but it could: as Peter is preparing to go back to Neverland and spinning tales like cotton candy for Wendy as a way to draw her back to him, Wendy turns to Mrs. Darling, begging her to let her leave with the boy. "But he does so need a mother," she says, to which *her* mother responds, "So do you, my love."

IV.

What would the story look like without a mother? Peter would die—wouldn't he? Or, if not die, he would surely be left to fend for himself in Neverland. But would that really be that bad? A future, older, hopefully more mature me will recognize that this is just what we tell ourselves to continue a threadbare, worn-out story of toxic caretaking and enabling. Peter wouldn't die without a mother and he wouldn't die without Wendy. Without either of them, however, he'd be left without someone to tell him stories, and this is the real heartbreaking truth.

Another heartbreaking truth: when Wendy first meets Peter Pan, she refuses to believe that the real reason he has come to her nursery isn't to see her, it's not even to retrieve his shadow. He has come to hear the stories:

> "Where are you going?" she cried with misgiving.
>
> "To tell the other boys."
>
> "Don't go, Peter," she entreated, "I know such lots of stories."
>
> Those were her precise words, so *there can be no denying that it was she who first tempted him.*
>
> He came back, and there was a greedy look in his eyes now which ought to have alarmed her, but did not.

According to the text, it was Wendy's fault. Her fault was steeped in her longing.

V.

In the most well-known photo of Sylvia Llewelyn Davies, she's reclining back on a stack of pillows, her head tilted to the side, a few dark curls falling into her face. The photograph was taken by J.M. Barrie, and on her face is a look that is both deeply sad and deeply resilient. The exhaustion in her eyes haunts me, because I know that where that exhaustion came from there was also still a spark or two left. If I recognize Sylvia as a tired, hurting woman that still has fight within her, the story doesn't seem so menacing.

But what if the look in her face is not something that naturally got captured? What if J. M. Barrie told her to look this way? What if this photo was taken to be a part of *his* story, and not hers? How would we ever know the truth of her story if not to finally let her create, to give her the space and the dignity to do so? To remember her for more than her sons, who inspired a different story?

Dreams also get kept in drawers. They get discarded, "put away," and forgotten, as Mrs. Darling explains to Wendy's younger brother, Michael. Being able to open the drawer where dreams are kept, admire them, and then put them away again is a special type of bravery, a bravery, we are told, that Mr. Darling has. But Mr. Darling also chains up Nana, the family dog and magical caretaker of his children, in the alleyway because he'd rather pretend she doesn't know how to look after his children than admit his own mistake.

Looking at dreams, admiring them, and then putting them back takes the bravery of stepping away from that which is harming you—if we take, for example, "dreams" to mean boys living in a fantastical land of underground houses and pirates, boys who never want to grow up. Of course, Peter is not a man abusing Mrs. Darling or Wendy, he's a child. And yet, the girls are the ones who have to grow up and leave.

Still, did Mrs. Darling have a choice? What made her leave Neverland and Peter? Her own mother, or her conscience?

The bravery of Mrs. Darling is never spoken of. Maybe because for her, it's survival.

Displacement

they want to cut me open over my already existing scar

I have recurring nightmares of my bare skin pressed against a metal operating table, the lights around me too bright, the sounds warping by the time the waves reach me, as if being forced into my consciousness through heavy cotton. In these nightmares, I am either crying or yelling or both, always spitting words at the doctor in the room, words that don't always take shape or form but that he seems to understand all the same: "All bodies are of equal value, whether they're fixed by the medical world or not." They are words of anger, but they are also words of fear, fear at the response they will elicit. I am either lying down or sitting when I say this, while the doctor is always standing, always towering above me. He will shake his head, then, with a knowing smile on his face and tell me, "No. No, they're not."

The doctors want to put more metal inside of me, cold and sterile and lifeless like the table beneath me. They want to cut me open over my already existing scar. I tell them no, that I already have a titanium rod fusing my spine, I don't need more incisions. They do not listen.

if my wheelchair is also my body

I am reminded of the differences between my body and the bodies of those around me every time I fly in a plane. My wheelchair is not allowed to board with me, and plane seats do not curve themselves to fit my specific curves. If my wheelchair is also my body, then I am suddenly without half of myself. And not just separated peacefully, but ripped apart—a tearing process that begins when airport security must take me aside to pat me down, maneuvering my limbs when I am unable to do so myself, because the metal in my back, not to mention the metal of my wheelchair, would set off the detector.

On the plane ride to Dublin, I stretch my halved body across the lap of the two helpers I brought with me. Because I am relatively small, and because contractures in my knees and hips mean that "fully stretched out" does not equal flat, I fit comfortably across my helpers' sets of legs. I try to sleep through the shifting night, but can't. Airports are never-places, and airplanes are even more so, especially when changing time zones means that time does not exist in the air the same way it does on the ground. Eventually, I give up on sleeping and read. I am going to Ireland for a six-week summer writing program through the University of Iowa. I distract myself from the discomfort of my body with words.

Before visiting Ireland, I spent years longing to be there, somehow believing that if I were in a new place, I would feel at home in my body. I held a belief, in my child and teenage mind clouded by anxiety and depression, that the earth, there, could heal me. Not heal my body, understand, but my itching desire to leave it. Even then, I wanted so badly to view the natural world as the balm so many claimed it to be, and even then, I had no idea how to balance my mechanical body—and by extension all the technology that I needed to live—with this desire.

When I arrive in Ireland that summer, I am confronted with a country and terrain that is uneven, broken, and inaccessible to wheels. The cobbled streets jar my body, and I have to drive down them in fits and spurts, allowing myself to recover from the bumpiness. The steps of buildings bar me from access, which means I am unable to enter many of the same places—restaurants, pubs, bookstores—that my peers explore after our classes together.

And yet—I realize while leaving the bus to tour Clonmacnoise, an abandoned monastery whose flush-with-the-ground gravestones I roll over, aware that I am putting my living body on top of the dead, that I feel a particular love for this unlikely home. *It is all too easy to fall in love in Ireland,* I think, just as I suspected, as a child, that it would be. As an adult, I still don't know the object of my desires, but I sense it has to do with the crisp air and the green pushing through the stones beneath my wheels that seem to signify a refusal to be buried. I realize the irony of my infatuation with this place and its people, considering how little of its physical makeup I could access. But our loyalties often defy logic, and our love always defies control.

I think our Clonmacnoise tour guide is overly charismatic, too charming, trying too hard to be funny. I'm in the minority in this (I would later listen to other members of the program gush over him), although Jessica, a fellow student who was roughly ten years senior to the rest of us early twenty-some-year-olds, agreed with me. Later, when we were all back in Dublin and Jessica, my helpers, and I were rehashing the trip over dinner, Jessica pointed her spoon at me from her spot by the sink. "He was weird, right?" I nodded, taking a bite of noodles.

But in that instant in Clonmacnoise, I know I'm in too marvelous a place to spend my time listening to this man's rehearsed history, and so I turn my wheelchair away from the crowd and leave, wandering away from the living and meandering through the dead. This, of course, is only an illusion, as the cemetery is overtaken with green, and the River Shannon curls its way just to the side, its water feeding the plants and the animals that had made Clonmacnoise their home, before moving along.

The excursion to Clonmacnoise is part of a weekend trip to Galway, a vibrant city known for its music and arts scene. Our entire program drove from Dublin on the East coast to Galway on the West, spilling out of the van that had been rented to visit the abandoned monastery, and then an abandoned church, and then a walled city. *Vans,* actually—a separate, accessible van had been rented for me to ride in with my helpers and a few others.

When we finally arrive in Galway, the hostel we are all staying at has steps from the lobby up to the floor where our rooms are. *They assured us it was accessible,* I'm told by the director of the program, and I realize their definition of "accessible" means a chair lift up the steps, or, if this does not accommodate your body, a back entrance directly adjacent to the garbage bins. Despite all of this, I am entranced, perhaps because

I am in a country not my own. If this happened in the US, I would be furious. Here, I think it is another part of the adventure.

"two long, cold thingammies"

One day, in our Irish poetry class, I open *The Wake Forest Book of Irish Women's Poetry* and a mermaid slips out, all angry chattering about being confined to the lines of a poem, sea water splashing onto my desk. This book has a black silhouette of a woman on its cover, flowers spewing from her open mouth, and a rounded stomach, perhaps growing life inside. This is our largest and heaviest book—a tome, our instructor called it—and yet it still could not contain this mermaid.

In its translation from Irish Gaelic to English by Paul Muldoon, Nuala Ní Dhomhnaill's "An Mhurúch san Ospidéal/The Mermaid in the Hospital" tells of a mermaid who wakes up to find her tail gone, replaced with "two long, cold thingammies." This mermaid is distraught, bewildered, heartbroken, even, to find her tail, that thing which allowed her to move so adeptly through water, completely missing. She doesn't understand her new, working legs because they are not her:

> *But here's the thing*
> *she still doesn't get—*
> *why she tumbled out after them*
> *arse-over-tip . . .*
> *How she was connected*
> *to those two thingammies*
> *and how they were connected*
> *to her.*

The sister who is attending to the mermaid in the hospital informs her what her new legs are for, that the loss of her tail is, in fact, not simply a cruel prank played by humans "legless with drink" (yes, *legless*).

The speaker of the poem—an unidentified voice who hovers just close enough to the mermaid to know her—has no choice, at the end, but to let her go: out of the hospital, into the world, atop two modes of mobility that were not made for her. This poem delivers a new iteration of meaning each time I read it, but my heart always aches at the ending:

> *In the long months*
> *that followed,*
> *I wonder if her heart fell*
> *the way her arches fell,*
> *her instep arches.*

boots on the ground

I am separated from my mechanical body again when we visit the Mini Cliffs, an outcrop of moonlike stones a short drive from their namesake, the Cliffs of Moher. I decide to get into the manual wheelchair-like stroller that we brought along, so that I can get closer to the ocean. Fi, a fellow student in the program who I would later connect with over chronic illness, came to sit on the ground beside me, and made a comment about the tiny purple flowers growing between the cracks in the rocks. The flower makes me think of the carved angel face hidden behind a pillar in a church we toured earlier that weekend—in a rage against iconography, Protestants had smashed all other stone angel faces in St. Nicholas's Church, missing this one because of its hiding spot. It wasn't supposed to be there, but it survived.

Now, my body is held by the purple cloth of the stroller, and I am looking down at tiny purple petals. For the first time since I can remember, my feet are touching the ground. Immediately after this trip, I will say the effect of seeing my feet touching the ground is reassuring. I'm not sure if *reassuring* is the correct word—*steadying*, perhaps. Or *triumphant*, although not triumphant in that I was no longer in my wheelchair, triumphant in a way that existed quietly inside me—I had managed to honor a younger self's desire to have my body flush with Ireland's terrain. I take one of my favorite photos of the entire trip right then, my black combat boots framed against the stone, the darkened craters in the rock ringed in green. Years later, I'll be in a creative nonfiction workshop with a theme of "Boots on the Ground"—that is, writing through wandering, that is, writing through walking, that is, the old and apparent greats who wrote meandering essays about, yes, meandering on their two legs, and so, perhaps in a moment of subconscious defiance, I included, in an essay I turned in for workshop, a description of the photo I took in Ireland of my black combat boots against the moon-stone and green grass. "I just have to say it," another student in the workshop said when I turned in that specific essay. "If the theme of this class is 'Boots on the Ground,' she did it. She actually gave us *boots on the ground*." And indeed I had, I realized. *Boots on the fucking ground.*

In Bray, a short train ride from Dublin, a group of us goes hiking along the side of the sea, the gray-blue sheen on the left of us, the sides of cliffs to our right. The path is mostly gravel, with patches of concrete every now and then. Like cobblestones, this isn't easy to drive on. I am exhausted by the end of our hike, and the loose stones have shaken free a screw from my rear tire, leaving the back end of my wheelchair bent until I returned to the US to have it fixed. Over the twenty-some years of having a power wheelchair, I have been told countless times by wheelchair repair people that the chair is not meant for such harsh and rocky terrain, as if it isn't the body I take with me wherever I go.

And that night on the coast of Ireland, while eating ice cream for dinner and looking out at the sea, I feel the heaviness invade my limbs that always precludes sickness.

I had been trained from twenty years of listening to my body to know what a dryness at the back of my throat means. The fear of getting sick and losing whatever semblance of control I have over my body kicks in the last week of being in Ireland, after I wake up in the middle of the night with a growing itch in the back of my throat, an itch that turns quickly to pain, and then to shallow, weak breaths. Once I am thrown into the ocean of my depression—the waves crashing my mind against the rough, jagged edges of the shore—there's only a tiny part of me that cares about even getting better. I become someone I want to crawl away from.

The student health doctor puts me on an aggressive antibiotic to stay on top of the congestion, something she only does because she knows my lungs are weak. My mom ends up flying back to Ireland to help me, and she walks into our communal kitchen area an hour or two after landing in Dublin. I'm eating mac-n-cheese, and the minute I see her, I start crying tears of relief. By the time we all fly back to the US, about a week later, I am no longer coughing, just dealing with an upset stomach from the antibiotics on an eight-hour flight, already having calculated what amount of liquid I could drink prior to flying, as there is no easy way for me to use the bathroom on a plane—calculations often referred to as "pee math" by other disabled people. Once again, I am estranged from my mechanical body while a fleeting illness is trapped within my body bound by skin.

I don't know why I latched onto Ireland in my childhood—maybe it was the fantasy books I read or the Celtic folk music my dad listened to—but from the minute our plane landed back in Chicago after the six weeks I had spent abroad, despite the homesickness churning in my stomach, there was a part of me that longed to go back immediately. The global spread of the COVID-19 pandemic flattened this longing out of me, as the UK and Ireland were faring no better than we were. But this was years before a particular deadly virus would reach across the lengths of the world, before it is estimated that 60 percent of COVID deaths in the UK are of disabled individuals, before Member of Parliament Charles Walker says, "We cannot cancel life to preserve every life," before Disability Action publishes a comprehensive report on the effects of COVID-19 on disabled people in Northern Ireland, which found increased concern about accessing medication, accessing care, and fears of being denied medical assistance if they were to contract COVID. This is, of course, a different story. When the pandemic hit, I realized I may never fly again, may never have to stretch myself out over the laps of my travel companions for particularly long flights, because I may never feel safe enough to do so.

Two years after leaving Ireland, during a heat-drenched Iowa summer, Fi and I work on a collection of short stories together that are inspired by the idea of being slightly out of whack. We wouldn't become close until this collaboration, even though, in Ireland, there was something that tied us together, whether it was the mermaid tattoos we both sported, the medical trauma we had both been through during our childhood, or the pieces we turned in for workshop, all of which seemed to feature a protagonist who was just slightly off-kilter (off-kilter, of course, being a matter of perspective).

"I think you two need to collaborate," the director of the study abroad program told us. Which we did, until Fi's hands began experiencing copious amounts of pain, barring him from typing for a solid month. "You could try dictation," I offered, though I would've been reluctant to take my own advice. The idea of having to breach the space of silence I create with myself and my writing, the solitude summoned when I enter into a back and forth between myself and the page—this is terrifying. Inserting my physical voice into this sphere is not appealing to me, but it could appeal to Fi. Is *appeal* the right word, or was it merely a matter of necessity?

Eventually it became less painful for Fi to type, and our collaboration returned to normal. *Our* normal, which, we had learned, could change at any second. My normal involved a wheelchair and needing help moving my arms, both things I was familiar with in my ritual of preparing to write. It did not involve speaking my words into existence on the page, but given the progressive and unpredictable nature of SMA, someday it might.

At some point that summer, Fi tells me, "What stands out about chronic medical problems is how you can feel fine and normal and then suddenly realize how thin the layer of protection is between you and the world."

overtaken with memories of water

Nuala Ní Dhomhnaill's mermaid grabbed hold of my heart that day in our classroom and never let go.

This mermaid goes through various stages in different poems, or, perhaps, is more than one mermaid—is one yet many, a whole community of merfolk who have left their homes in the sea but have lost the language to express, fully, what happened to them. One poem, "Admhail Shuaithinseach/A Remarkable Admission," reveals that the merfolk had perhaps undergone "some sort of ethnic cleansing," a nod to the atrocities—explicit and subtle—at work in our real world. These mermaids, then, were forcibly removed from their homes because of their very bodies, their very being—they were ripped from their homes because of who they were.

In the poem sequence that follows the life of our mermaid, she never seems to catch a break. She's seduced, killed, brought back to life, and eventually ends up back where she began, in a hospital. She is not happy here, and the speaker of the poems mourns this lost happiness. The mermaid is someone "who laughed, so far as I can remember, / three times only when she was on dry land."

And her daughter? Her daughter, who is born of her mother in human form and thus has legs and no tail, is overtaken with memories of water, water that "starts at her feet and ankles / and slides further and further up / over her thighs and hips and waist." And her daughter has no word for this feeling, for water, no point of reference, but she is haunted by what her mother lost, and despite having no language to describe this, she still doesn't feel whole. Because a mermaid is no longer a mermaid without her tail. And of course, it is just as silly to think that a mermaid can be contained by a poem, that a feeling or experience or life can be described by a word.

I imagine that this mermaid has recurring nightmares as well—nightmares of waking up in the hospital bed to find the part of her that made her who she is, the part of her that made her different than the white coats giving her blank stares over clipboards, that beautiful, slippery, scaly part of her gone.

DREAM

The Victim

You have a dream one night that you are getting a miracle serum injected into your spinal fluid. It doesn't feel like a hospital because the floors are carpeted and the walls are muted and you're not actually being sliced open against your will. A figure in a cloak is with you, and you are both listening to the doctors, and someone is telling you that the serum will likely leak into your lungs and crawl up your throat because of gravity being canceled on an operating table and it will mix with your saliva and you will choke on it like a pebble turned to gritty liquid between your teeth.

You have a dream one night that you are in a room in a hospital with too-bright lights and too-cold metal and walls that seem to close in around you every time you look away. It's like the frog being boiled alive in water that increases temperature microscopically, never enough for it to notice until it's too late—the twist here is that you notice but you can't do anything about it.

You have a dream one night that you are standing (floating) in a cavernous room, an art gallery of sorts, spotlights on sculptures giving the walls a green hue. The sculptures are bodies, you think. They feel like negative space in this room, like they're antimatter, sucking everything that weighs *something* toward them and into them and through them. There's a row of molds, torsos only, stuck atop poles at chest height. You ~~don't fit inside of them~~ can't make yourself fit comfortably against their ~~skin~~ clay, they swallow you whole. There's a doctor somewhere saying they ~~can~~ will make you into a sculpture to be placed in the entryway of the gallery, a specimen to draw onlookers in, like the girl with webbed hands trapped in a tank of water outside the carnival tent.

MERMAID INTERLUDE

The First Mermaid

Becoming mermaid was a choice. For me, but not for everyone.

This is how it happened: I moved in with the parents of—surprise!—the man I was engaged to marry. He was away. He was always away. He felt that my moving in with his parents would make up for his absence to all of us. His parents were rigid types, although their rigidity seemed mirrored in all the humans around me. Please don't ask why I agreed to marry him. There is a headiness involved in choosing, after all.

One night, his parents and I were sitting around the dining room table, spooning food into our mouths and pretending to enjoy each other's company when his mom—my mother-to-be—said something about worrying about her son, and his dad said, "Jesus Christ, he's fine," and I thought, suddenly, *Oh My God, did all our foremothers marry men who don't know how to communicate?*

The answer was and is and will likely continue to be yes. It felt like a particularly human problem, this failure to communicate. Another problem unique to humans: believing they are the only ones with an intelligent form of communication. Still, even for mermaids, there are so many things words can't do, or that we can't figure out how to fit into a collection of letters.

I left his parents' house the next day, making an appointment with the surgeon to have my legs replaced with the slippery tail of a fish—I wasn't committing to a full transformation, understand, just halfway, just enough to no longer claim humanity as my own. Still, transformation was not a one and done thing. The surgeon did not lop off my legs, stitching a giant tail to my hips. She severed tendons, sewed in the beginnings of pelvic fins. From there, the rest of the metamorphosis occurred on its own. The surgeon didn't ask questions, just bid me a terse "Be careful." Whispers of mermaid eradication were already circulating the kingdom, though nothing had officially been proclaimed. To willfully make myself a target was surely insanity, I know. But remember what I said about choosing?

Oh yes, of course, you want to know why his parents worried about my betrothed (I never married him, but surely you already knew that). Well, he was a revolutionary, publicly claiming the king's tyranny, and the ways in which we as subjects were complicit in our own systematic degradation, the systematic degradation of the land. We assumed this was why he was always gone. Maybe my leaving and willful transformation was actually a way for me to skirt around the edges of the responsibility he was always going on about. Maybe in shirking the complicity I became complicit. It's not something I try to understand.

It did make me wonder, though, where the revolution was actually meant to start, given that this man's relationship with his mom was tenuous at best—for a while, I figured his biting comments were symptomatic of actual anger toward his mom, but eventually I was forced to face the reality of a man so doubled over in grand views of world change that he missed the ways in which the world inside his home was shattering.

When I did start to change—when I started to feel pricks of pain in my butt and legs and then looked down to see tiny scales beginning to push their way through my skin where the fins had been planted—the witch was the first one I told. She was known for her golden thread and homegrown tinctures—her weaves provided more comfort and warmth than was scientifically feasible for the fineness of her thread, and the potions she brewed were simple herbs that worked better than what our doctors would prescribe us. Not that any of this was surprising: the magic in her creations, and the fact that I loved her so deeply. She gave me a salve for my skin to ease the tenderness brought on from transformation.

"It makes sense," she told me, handing over the jar in which the lotion she had made was stored. "You are becoming the wild inside of yourself—manifesting a departure from the norm." And though my heart swelled at this, I could tell from the way her eyes shimmered that she was sad at her words. I was leaving her before we had ever even allowed ourselves to dissolve into one another.

Of course I loved her. That I loved her was never in question, and I refuse to even deliberate what counted as love during our time together and what didn't. I knew to avoid certain topics, such as the last person I had fucked, the way the press of the last woman's lips made me feel. I didn't talk about any of this, not after the first time I brought up another woman, the woman I had gone home with the night before. At that news, the witch grew quiet, suddenly, her hands stilled on the loom and the blanket she was weaving, yarn spilling onto the floor.

"I'll make some tea, then," she said, after my acknowledgement that I had slept with the woman down the road, a woman we both knew, the night before. I bit my lip in frustration and looked away from her. The frustration, understand, was all toward myself.

Notes From a Class on Trauma

1 Assuming, then, that trauma has a voice.

2 Assuming, then, that trauma is a wounding: the incision made down my back when I was eight years old.

3 Assuming, then, trauma as a result of the wound: the insistent terror I encounter in the face of "I consent," the hazy feeling in my body during other medical procedures, my writing.

4 Assuming, then, that the body itself provides the link: It can become difficult to hold both these truths simultaneously: Without spinal fusion surgery at eight years old, you would have died and you don't want to die. You also don't want your disease to magically disappear. When you think of the body as a link, you think of the body as the answer, or at the very least, an answer. You also think of your friend who had a similar disease to yours and who died when you were a freshman in high school after her parents took her off life support. What percentage of the circumstances leading up to her death were rooted in her body? What circumstances were not?

5 Assuming, then, that this is not an exaggeration: You cannot remember the first time you saw a romantic relationship involving a disabled individual represented in the media. Maybe 2016—the release of *Me Before You* coincided with your first realization that you have panic attacks, dissociation your most recognizable symptom. You sat outside your grandparent's house and cried, feeling as if you were floating right above your body, and that the flowers in their backyard, the cement of their patio, the wood of the ramp that traversed the step into their house—all of these were not real. It took you a while before you could talk, but you finally answered your mom's question of what was wrong by saying, "There's a movie that just came out where the disabled protagonist falls in love with his helper and then he kills himself at the end." You don't know how to shake off the inheritance of these stories.

6 Assuming, then, that the individual cannot be separated from the collective.

7 Assuming, then, that there is no guilt-free speech: I don't want to write disability as tragedy; I also don't want to leave parts of the story out. Also all in 2016, the year *Me Before You* came out—an employee at a care facility for disabled individuals in Japan writes a letter stating, "I envision a world where a person with multiple disabilities can be euthanized, with an agreement from the guardians, when it is difficult for the person to carry out household and social activities." He later murders nineteen disabled individuals living in this facility and injures twenty-six more. Julianna Snow, a five-year-old with a form of Muscular Dystrophy, tells her parents she doesn't want to go back to the hospital the next time she is sick and wants to go to heaven instead. Her parents oblige and she dies. Fourteen-year-old Jerika Bolen, who had the same disease you have, decides to end her life, citing intense pain as the reason, pain that was unable to be effectively managed. There is a "last dance" held in her honor. Two important components of Jerika's identity that are often overlooked: she was black, and she was openly queer.

8 Assuming, then, that trauma marks the body: The scar down the middle of your back should not be read as a signifier of social trauma, but rather as a mark of privilege that you have access to and can afford this medical procedure.

9 Assuming, then, a pattern of non-consent.

10 Assuming, then, a pattern of non-consent: The realization that your body isn't yours might come to you instantaneously, in the moment that four residents file into the room behind the doctor, and you're sitting on the table with your shirt off, slouched to the side because that's how your muscles work and that's what they're all here to see. Of course, the doctor asked you and your parents if it was okay for the students to observe, and of course you and your parents said yes. You are six years old. You don't understand how consent works. You understand that you have the *ability* to say no, but you exercise this mainly in what one might consider normal six-year-old activities, such as playing imaginary friends with your brother, or not giving up a certain crayon at school. This isn't exactly what one would consider a normal six-year-old activity, is it? Being looked at by doctors and medical students in this way?

11 Assuming, then, a pattern of non-consent: Something happens to you when you are (you think) in second grade. When making drinks at your apartment with A., the girl you are dating, you tell her about the abusive helper you had your freshman year of undergrad, the gaslight-y, manipulative friend but more than friend from a year or so ago, and then you say something that you surely only say because of the alcohol inside of you: "There was this incident with a man when I was little. I'm still stepping around it and only recently realizing how much that experience shaped me." You don't say anything more than that; your instances of trauma feel inconsequential next to hers, and you don't want to undermine her experiences with details of how your helper at that time—who worked for the elementary school you went to and stayed with you all day—had carried you out of the bathroom after helping you and placed you in the lap of a man you detested (you don't know why you had such a strong aversion to him, but your guess would be that he made you feel small and helpless and insignificant). Once you realized you were being carried out of the bathroom to be

placed on his lap, you started screaming and crying, which somehow cruelly mixed with the laughter of your helper. You think the man was laughing too. You were wearing shiny blue pants, like second graders do. This is all you remember of this experience, but you did not want to go to school after that, and your mom had to assure you each morning that this man wouldn't be there—what does this mean? The point of telling all of this now, though, is not to illustrate how your mind or memory went blank after you had been placed in his lap (you have always been, for the most part, physically at the mercy of others), but how the intricacies of this memory are not ones you want to divulge to the girl you are dating. You don't want to tell her all of this, you want to kiss her. You want to curl your body into hers.

12 Assuming, then, an impossible dichotomy: the imperative to tell versus the impossibility of telling. What Audre Lorde meant when she wrote "Your silence will not protect you"—not that bystander's complicity will circle around to harm them (although, surely, it will), but that our own omissions will not end up keeping us safe.

13 Assuming, then, that trauma fractures linearity: Time behaves oddly in response to bodies being stolen. It splinters and warps, bubbles and collapses in on itself. For just this moment, though, entertain the notion of time as straightforward, and learn to go back. Go back years to your mother giving up her job as a graphic designer to raise your brother and you, decades to your grandmother forming ten children from her own body, centuries to the farmers' wives being defined in relation to their husbands, eons to the women who kept their children alive, who kept their families alive, who did what they had to do which sometimes meant, you'll come to understand, sacrificing parts of themselves for others. Sometimes, the parts of themselves that they have no choice but to sacrifice *are* their children—the ones whose lungs are too weak and filled with fluid, the ones who cannot see, the deaf ones, the lame ones, the ones who twitch and scream and cannot vocalize their understanding of the world in front of them, who cannot, for instance, say no. But, of course, these children never did belong to their mothers, just as you will come to recognize that your body, along with not belonging to you, also does not belong to the woman who birthed you. During the years that you teeter between childhood and loosely defined adulthood, (*loosely defined* because if adulthood equals autonomy surely adulthood is a lie), you spend a lot of time wondering if girls are born already shrouded in armor with knives for hands, and if so, do they tear up their mothers' insides on their way into the world or do the gouges only make their mothers' bodies stronger?

14 Assuming, then, that trauma fractures time: When you say, *The girl I'm dating*, you'll stop mid-sentence, wonder at your need to continue to refer to women as girls—is it because you, yourself, feel stuck in a perpetual girlhood? Is it because of the perceived infantility that haunts disabled individuals well past their infancy? Alcoholics stop maturing after their first drink, time stops turning after a body is stolen, if a body was never *not* stolen, does time pass for the woman living in said body?

15 Assuming, then, that trauma entails leaving: A body without fear is a body refusing to harbor the belief you will only be known in your abandonment. A body without fear is a body that does not have to do anything besides exist to keep others from leaving it. If you need to have left the traumatic experience or site of the traumatic experience seemingly unscathed, *seemingly* becomes the word you latch onto.

16 Assuming, then, bodies as stories: During undergrad, you work on an investigative journalism piece cataloging the abuse of people with disabilities and learn this—In the time period of January to June 2014 alone, there were 3,161 reports of dependent adult abuse made to the Iowa Department of Human Services.

17 Assuming, then, that narratives produce catharsis.

18 Assuming, then, the need for collective memory work: The disability community will never agree on how to talk about the deaths—of Julianna, of Jerika, of so many—because the disability community is made up of individuals, all with differing perspectives and different histories of hurt. You didn't know Julianna Snow or Jerika Bolen (You had met Jerika once, actually, at a conference—the narrative isn't that neat). You didn't know their bodies, you couldn't know their pain. You would like to hold these two truths simultaneously: As a child, during a particularly terrible battle with a respiratory infection, like Julianna, you had begged your parents to let you die, and you are lucky (surely this is the right word, as precarious as disabled life seems to be) that they had not obeyed your wishes. At the same time, the amount of ongoing, physical pain that Jerika talked about you have no experience with (the acute physical pain you've experienced from medical procedures are isolated in their acuteness and intensity to the time of the procedure. The pain following your spinal fusion surgery is hazy—you know it was there, but have only flashes of memory of it). It seems cruel to silence her voice even more than it was systemically silenced as a black, queer, disabled woman by saying she should not have been allowed to end her life.

19 Assuming, then, the erasure of the body: You want to honor Julianna's and Jerika's bodily experiences, their bodily pain, their bodily fear, while still questioning what was at work to make it so easy for them to choose to die. Is a choice really a choice if you're being told over and over again that your life is not worth living, that you are a burden to your caregivers? Is it a choice if you're fourteen years old? Five years old? Eight? The traumas don't match, the choices don't match, the pain is not commensurate, how could we even think they are commensurate? But what choices need to be made to keep living?

20 Assuming, then, there is no definitive settlement, no resolution: You could never quite figure out—still cannot quite figure out—what happened after you were carried out of the bathroom in second grade and placed on the man's lap.

Breath

We didn't talk much about my surgery before it happened, or if we did, I simply blocked it out.

The night before my parents and I reported for pre-op at University of Iowa Hospitals and Clinics, we stayed at the Ronald McDonald House, a kid-centered hotel-like lodging near the hospital for families whose children were going through medical treatments. A family friend of ours, who was also a nurse and had been one of my helpers, came to visit us there, as she lived in Iowa City by this time. I played in the backyard of the Ronald McDonald House with other kids as she and my mom talked, and I tried to shut out any knowledge of what lay on the other side of that night. If I tried hard enough, squinted my eyes so the streetlights became stars, I could pretend that I was simply on a fun vacation, or at a special summer camp for kids whose bodies moved a little bit differently than everyone else's.

I have one other sharply distinct memory of the future of surgery crashing into my present. I am walking down the hallway of my house, *walking* not a stand-in word, wearing my orthopedic braces which straightened my hips and knees, scooting along with my walker. I am on my way from somewhere to another, and my mom is talking about me wearing my bi-pap mask, which is designed to help me take deeper breaths, at night. I am not used to the way the mask sits on my face or the way the air enters my lungs, and because of this, I don't like it. I shake my head no.

"Okay, but we'll have to work on wearing it soon," my mom says. "Your surgery is in July, and you'll need to wear it when you're recovering from that."

I can see my younger self's face twist into a look of frustration, lips pursed and to the side, eyebrows furrowed. But I don't believe I said anything in response to this, because there was nothing to say. I'm sure I put the looming summer month out of my mind and continued down the hallway, shifting my weight from one leg to the other, moving forward in barely measurable increments.

Two years after my surgery, at an actual summer camp for kids whose bodies moved a little bit differently, I met Caroline. She was the cool, boy-crazy, older sister who would later move to the same town I lived in, which happened to have a plethora of group homes and services for kids with disabilities. At this camp, kids would have a one-on-one counselor to help them with their personal care if they needed it, otherwise the campers who needed less help would share counselors between them. I brought my own helper with me, unwilling to surrender my care to a stranger for a week. In this, I was lucky and privileged.

My usual camp counselor was pregnant one year, too pregnant to help me, and so I had a different helper come with me that week. There was something slightly off about this dynamic the entire time I was there; in part because she did not know my camp friends like my usual counselor did, and in part because she and another camp counselor flirted with each other in stolen moments that they thought we didn't see, but that I very much picked up on. Once, while my helper was carrying me out of the swimming pool, he came over and "helped" her carry me, by placing his hands on the bare skin of my back. His touch, and the obviousness with which he was using me to get to her, made me sick.

The fact that other campers had to have strangers touch them—although within a different context—was not lost on me. Disabled writer and activist Mia Mingus coined the term "forced intimacy" to explain how disabled people have to bare themselves physically and emotionally, whether they want to or not, in order to access care they need in order to survive. Although I didn't have the language for this experience at the time, forced intimacy was something I was both personally familiar with and witnessed for a week each summer, until I aged out of camp.

One night in our cabin, as everyone was getting ready for bed, a few counselors came in to help Caroline use her cough assist machine—another breathing machine we both had and which forced you to take deep breaths, keeping your lungs elastic. Like Caroline, I had brought my cough assist machine to camp with me and used it routinely each morning and night. Unlike Caroline, I had a machine that was a newer model with automatic settings, and I had someone helping me use it each morning and night who knew me and, by extension, knew the routine. I did not have to explain to my counselor how to work my adaptive equipment, nor did I have to negotiate with her when I was going to use it.

That night, though, I sat propped up in my camp bed, wearing my bi-pap mask, reading whichever book I had brought with me that week. My usual counselor, who was back with me that year after having a kid, had gone to the counselors' quarters to get ready for bed herself. I was left to be the room's observer, making jokes with the other girls in our cabin in between reading paragraphs in my book. But when the group of counselors came in to help Caroline, including one of the women who was in charge of that week at camp, I stopped focusing on the flurry of activity stemming from the rest of our cabin and watched as these women walked to Caroline's bed, talked with her briefly, and then turned the cough assist machine on.

Caroline was propped up in her bed like I was, and because her cough assist machine did not have automatic settings, the counselors helping her had to count to three while flipping the switch to inhale, and then three again after flipping the switch to exhale. I hated this, the inherent inaccuracy of relying on someone new each night and morning to count to three at the same speed.

And then in between breaths of the machine, suddenly: "Why are you slouching, Caroline?" It was the voice of the woman in charge of this week of camp.

"I'm not slouching!" Caroline said, and because she would have been somewhere between thirteen and fifteen at this time, her voice held the edge of a whiny teenager, an edge which surely dug at these counselors, except it was an edge that she had sharpened and sharpened and sharpened in order to survive, and I was about to witness her own survival used against her, the caging in of my friend, someone who came to camp each year without the steadfast group of supporting family members that dropped me off, without a consistent helper like the one I brought with me despite Caroline needing more intensive care than I did, without equipment that was best suited to help her.

"You are slouching," the woman repeated. "Didn't you just have surgery on your back to make you sit up straight? I'm sure Dr. Weinstein wouldn't be very happy with you if he knew you were slouching." The same back surgery I had had at eight years old, performed by the same doctor, who, I thought, could not give a flying fuck if Caroline and I still leaned slightly to one side because the spinal fusion procedure did not mean a bone straight spine, it meant a spine that curved less than it had before it was melded to metal, and thus lungs which would no longer be crushed.

"I'm *not* slouching," Caroline repeated.

I kept my book open in my lap, although if this was the satisfying short story of a young girl speaking up for her friend against a world that viewed them as perpetual children, I would have carefully closed the book and set it aside, before clearing my throat to speak through my own breathing machine, which I still did, which still shifted the energy in the room, but not to a degree that was enough.

"The surgery doesn't make your back perfectly straight," I said. "I had it done when I was eight and my back is still curved. She's not slouching."

The woman looked at me, and Caroline looked at me, and years later, as I sat in front of my bedroom window imagining the glass shattering around my bloody fist after knowing I had lost her, I would think, *My God, how we have failed you.*

The heat of July crept closer. As fierce and determined as I believed myself to be, I could not stop time. And so, as I began to comprehend what lay in this future set out for me by doctors, I came up with a plan to evade this.

A scene I would play over and over in my mind at night, as I lay in darkness facing the wall of my room: the same exam room, the same doctor plus a few more, and me—little, defiant me—telling them that if they proceeded with the surgery, I would simply hold my breath until I died. I was learning the power of breath, fighting the loss of lung capacity with intentional loss of breathing, and in my imagined story, which I armed myself with in the coming months like a blade hidden in my pant leg, I controlled the ending.

I truly don't know if I understood, at this age, that without surgery to straighten my spine I would probably not live very long, anyway.

Of course, I never made good on my threat. I never even voiced the threat, until years and years later when I told this story of eight-year-old me to the man I thought I loved. The man I thought I loved laughed, and of course my heart and body recoiled at his laugh, a sound which usually made the pit of my stomach burn. But still, of course, I ignored this.

There was a time, once, when my breathing machines saved my life. That is, I was sure I was dying from lack of breath (part panic attack, part severe congestion in weak lungs) and my cough assist pushed the air back into my lungs, over and over, and my bi-pap helped the speed of my breaths to slow down, the gasps turn to measured inhales and exhales, until I was able to close my eyes and rest.

I was so certain I was close to death. And I both wanted to embrace the end and did not. I wanted the struggle to draw air into my lungs to be over, but I also very much wanted to live. But I think, maybe, I wanted the terror and physical stress to end more.

I've read stories of characters being spared death only after they've surrendered to it. But this isn't a story, except to an extent, and I'm not a character, except when I make myself one. I surrendered and was spared, but others weren't. And how cruel, for a god to dole out death to someone who so badly wants to live.

When I graduated from the University of Iowa with my bachelor's, we had to park next to the Ronald McDonald House. Graduates then had to make their way to Carver-Hawkeye Arena, where the ceremony was being held. I had half of my head shaved at this point in my life, and so the graduation cap that I had painted with "Make America THINK Again" and a raised fist inside the female Venus symbol could only be pinned on one side of my head.

I didn't realize what the brick brown building was until I saw the sign, because it was so much more colorful, yet somehow muted, in my memories. *Ronald McDonald House Charities, Eastern Iowa.* It was somehow smaller than I had remembered it, which I guess makes sense—not only was I younger and smaller when I had last been here, but that place, like the hospital, had pushed itself beyond the borders of my mind that night before my surgery. These places were, to an extent, larger than life.

I visited camp twice while I was living in Iowa City, somewhat of a homecoming. Like the Ronald McDonald House, the grounds of the camp seemed smaller. There were some campers there who I still knew, who had been much younger than I was—maybe six or seven—when they first started coming. Now, they were getting ready to graduate camp, and the campers who were closer to my age when I graduated were there as counselors, living elsewhere, or gone.

And yet, nothing had changed. Or everything had.

There is a photo of me as a child on the desk in my childhood bedroom, a photo which never fails to delight me. In it, I am wearing bright blue and yellow overalls—the sky and the sun in one piece of fabric—and I am sticking my tongue out at whoever is behind the camera. It's a joyful tongue-sticking-out, not one of feigned anger. My brown eyes are smiling.

I know it's a bit self-indulgent to find so much pleasure in a photograph of oneself, but I spent so many years after that photo was taken seeing ugly whenever I looked in the mirror. My older cousin sent me that photo with one of herself from that same year, her hair spiked and lips shiny with lip gloss. They hung on my apartment wall in Iowa City for years, an apartment this same older cousin would drive to on weekends to help me, family and helper rolled into one.

She would, each night, place the bi-pap mask on my nose. By this point in my life, thirteen years after I surrendered to using this machine each time I went to bed, my nose is reshaped from the mask being pressed into my nostrils for hours on end, so different from the button nose in the photo of me on my desk.

Also, by this point: The air from the bi-pap tastes sweet every night, and I no longer see ugly reflected in glass. What I see, now, is more like the sunflower sky emblazoned on the chest of a younger me, and as it rises and falls, a sun as it rises and sets.

Bruise as Signifier

it never looked as terrible as it felt / for this i could never forgive my body

Before I traded in Iowa for Kansas as my definition of home and uprooted myself to a new state for graduate school, the boundary between my body and the world I moved through shifted in two distinct ways:

In May, three years earlier, shortly after returning home to Iowa from a trip I took to San Francisco with a friend and my cousin Sarah, the chair that I use to shower tipped forward on its trip back into my bedroom, and I fell. The wheels had gotten caught on a snarl of carpet, and although the helper that was pulling the chair was able to stop my head from hitting the floor, my legs absorbed most of the impact from the fall. Suddenly in a position to stare up at the ceiling, this is exactly what I felt: cold, then hot, a pulsing in my veins and my voice didn't quite come out either, there was a wobble to my "It's going to be alright, it's going to be alright"—assurances as much to myself as to my helper who was crying above me, now. Although my right leg, the one that was most injured, swelled a bit and took on a purple, and then green hue, it never looked as terrible as it felt. For this, I could never forgive my body.

Also—plans moved forward for me to get a new wheelchair, a Levo Combi, a special chair made in Switzerland that can recline and stand up. I had gotten my first Levo Combi in fourth grade, my second as a sophomore in high school, and now, was battling insurance to get a new one. Codes had changed, apparently, in the last sixish years. American wheelchair companies, such as Permobil, were now making chairs that did—for all intents and purposes—the same thing as Levos. And because of this, insurance would no longer cover them.

It does the same thing as your old wheelchair, the reps from Permobil kept telling me about the chair I had agreed to try. Even the people who worked at the medical supply and repair store said this, and if you looked at the two wheelchairs side by side, without my body in either one, it would be hard to argue with this. The end result: their reclined and elevated positions were essentially the same. But this was an *end result*—the path that the two chairs took to get to this point were all together quite different, a difference I had difficulty articulating in words, but that my body understood implicitly.

To explain all of this to the Permobil reps and wheelchair repair people involved contorting my body into increasingly uncomfortable positions in front of their eyes—demonstrating to them how the Permobil wheelchair made my body floppy and slouched, the semblance of control I have while in a wheelchair that melds itself to my curves shattered by the specific way these gears and hydraulics moved. It was a feeling similar to sitting in an airplane seat, completely dependent on outside supports that are not there.

"You know, I think I get it," the Permobil rep said to me one day during a trial run, kneeling down beside me in his tucked-in button-up shirt and khakis. "My wife and I talk about experiential knowing versus practical knowing—this is experiential knowing." I was pleasantly shocked by his admission and smiled.

"Yes," I said. "Exactly."

Finally, we made videos explaining the difference in wheelchairs, elicited letters from the Permobil reps who agreed their chair would not work for me and sent everything to insurance. Insurance finally caved.

pain is not always commensurate with injury

My body is read differently in Kansas than it is in Iowa, another fact that forces the boundary between self and surrounding to shift. To receive Spinraza in Iowa, I must agree to have a hole drilled through the titanium rod fused to my spine, as the drug has to be injected directly into my spinal fluid. In Kansas, however, this is no longer necessary. My spinal structure is interpreted quite differently by doctors roughly 300 miles south.

And then, of course, there are the questions which never stop coming.

The questions asked annually by someone evaluating me for insurance purposes: "Do you require partial, complete, or no assistance with dressing and bathing?"

The questions asked by organizations funding my care about what I'm going to do when their agency pulls support: "What other long-term funding options do you have for your personal care attendant hours?"

And, of course, the questions asked by doctors: "Do you think you've gotten stronger?" or "Have you noticed any improvements?"

My answer to the last question has not changed over the past year. "I think I'm able to move my right arm on and off my armrest easier than I was before," although more recently there has also been this addition: "I think I'm able to project my voice louder and for longer." Both of these, however, end with the qualifier: "But it's hard to say for certain, I'm not really sure."

At the end of January 2020, as I was lying in a hospital bed waiting to be wheeled back for my next injection of Spinraza, the nurse that was working replied with something I had yet to hear from anyone else: "Well it's your body. If you notice you can do something now that you couldn't before, there's not any question about it." She had short hair and a husky voice, and I realized in that moment how easily I could become attracted to her. *Anecdotally*, I thought, *look how far we've come since theorists first identified doctors dismissing patients' symptoms as a problem.* Of course, anecdotally, if parts of this story shifted, things may not seem to have come as far after all.

The bruises which flowered on my left arm are physical evidence of the needles that entered to find my blood or feed me painkillers, while the right side of my torso that takes in the 5- to 8-inch-long needle that goes to my spine rarely changes appearance, never discolors to a bruise. If *bruise* is a signifier of a deeper hurt—if *deeper hurt* is the signified, does the signified no longer exist without the signifier? No, obviously not. Except, except, except.

Halfway through my first November in Kansas, I stopped sleeping, and by "stopped sleeping" I mean I stole hours throughout the night, but never enough, dozing in fits. If the loss of sleep was caused by first semester grad school stress and realizing I had feelings for a friend who was in the middle of a long-distance relationship with her boyfriend, it resulted in a headache the morning of injection number I don't know how many, before I was even wheeled back to the room in which I would be slid into a CT machine before having my side punctured. Although I chugged coffee the minute the procedure was done and lay flat for an hour in the waiting area I had been assigned to (standard post-injection practices), by the time I was downstairs getting ready to leave the hospital, my head was in a state of pain that can only be described metaphorically: splitting, pounding, bones caving in.

The spinal headache is a phenomenon that occurs, as I understand it, when fluid from the spine leaks from the puncture site on the spinal column and creates pressure in places it's not meant to be. "As I understand it" is another qualifier, meant to soften the edges of what we can expect from language. I looked through the bluish glass of the hospital's front bay window and thought, *I'm having a spinal headache,* which was quickly followed by, *I'm about to have a panic attack.*

"I think I have a spinal headache," I said as the nurses hooked me back up to the monitors and I lay flat on the bed with a blanket over me while my eyes squeezed out a continual stream of tears. *And a panic attack,* words I thought but didn't say, words that pushed up against the wall that had descended inside of me between myself and the outside world. I used to describe these experiences as the opposite of panic attacks, because instead of expanding outwardly in panic, I shrunk inward, retreating from myself until my body became a shell and I stopped believing what I saw in front of me was real. Technically, according to my therapist in Iowa and her DSM-5, this is still a panic attack, and I guess I have used this term as a stand-in for what I don't know how to label, what I don't know how to say happened.

"Your writing is never flowery or overly descriptive," a creative writing professor once told me. What I think she meant, what I think I mean, is that I care deeply about the weight behind a word, that I want precision.

What did happen that day, unquestionably and with no more fanfare than what normally accompanies a group of people in white coats sweeping into a room, is that that doctor who'd injected me said what I was experiencing was indeed *not* a spinal headache, as those occur usually a day or two after a spinal tap is performed, not directly following a procedure. But a girl I know gets spinal headaches frequently after her injections, or at least I thought.

a hazy feeling of uncertainty i couldn't even name

Despite its easy seductiveness, I know what the nurse tells me that day about my body isn't true. There's a difference, after all, between paying attention to what your body tells you (do our bodies speak?) and interpreting it correctly.

Case in point: About a year and a half after I begin receiving injections of Spinraza, the fingers on my left hand begin to act up, cramping into curled positions, perhaps as a result of the tingling running down my arm, a new sensation I woke up with one morning. The recent development of my left arm and hand was thankfully temporary, as there is no question it would impact my day-to-day life—as I was typing thoughts on my phone, that morning, the cramping in my thumb caused an intermittent heaviness that resulted in a dragging of digits across the keyboard. Wrong letter here, too many spaces here—my right thumb comes in to correct the mistakes made, but you see where the confusion lies. Is my left arm feeling the effects of an issue related to my nerves, or my muscles? Are they not connected? Meanwhile, my right arm continues to get stronger, but ultimately I prefer to have function in my fingers, as this is needed to type, which is needed to write, which is needed for me to create and thus to live.

Have you noticed any improvements? Well, we'd have to agree on the definition of "improvements," first.

I'm in my apartment in Kansas, and the shadows are lengthening on the walls and my cat is rubbing his face up against my feet on my footrest and I can feel the lump rising in the back of my throat and my mind threatening to leave my body.

"What's wrong, Hannah?" my helper, who has miraculously learned to read my emotions, asks.

I'm scared it's not working, I think, and then say, in regard to Spinraza.

"Hey, it's okay," my helper says. "You're not getting worse, right?"

I wasn't, but the experience of the injections was becoming a lot for me to go through for a hazy feeling of uncertainty I couldn't even name.

i keep waiting for the burning twinge in the pit of my stomach

The body, the boundaries keep shifting. I want my body to be able to talk to me, with words that my mind can comprehend. Lucy Grealy asks in her memoir *Autobiography of a Face* (also a founding text in disability studies), "Language supplies us with ways to express ever subtler levels of meaning, but does that imply language *gives* meaning, or robs us of it when we are at a loss to name things?" I'm trying, every day, to answer this question.

"I'm not sure this piece is actually about who you think it's about," the same creative writing professor who mentioned my leaning toward unflowery language once told me. I had thought it was about the girl who made me realize I was queer—I had poured all my hurt and anger over her rejection into an essay written in the second person, detailing our friendship and flirting and falling apart. I'd addressed this piece to the girl, choosing to have the *you* as a stand-in for her, not myself. My professor thought the essay was about me. It was, of course, about both, as it is also about every girl I fell for after.

Fear and desire feel awfully similar, I realize, which is perhaps why it takes me such a long time to understand that my churning stomach and clammy skin before going on dates with men is a side effect of my anxiety around intimacy with men, not butterflies. But now, even after I've come to identify as gay and understand that my intimacy-with-men-induced anxiety is not, in fact, something I need to work through, I still wonder where the line between desire and fear falls.

During the fall semester in my second year of grad school, I became consumed with a girl I came to refer to as Moon-Hair Girl because of the way the moonlight would fall on her dark hair. We met for the first time at a cat-themed store (because some things aren't surprising), and then she bought me tea at the coffee shop next door while we played board games and traded facts about ourselves. This woman elicited a nervousness within me that cramped my insides, reminiscent of the first day of my period. During those months, I worried about saying the right thing, about doing the wrong thing, about not being beautiful enough or witty enough or strong enough to move my hands and my body in the ways that are expected of me. When she didn't respond to my texts for hours and then days at a time, I worried it was my fault, not something happening on her end. It eventually ended because I wanted more, and she didn't.

Later, months and months later, when I'm stuck at home in Iowa due to the COVID-19 pandemic, I meet a new woman, O., on a dating app. She tends plants in the same town where both my parents went to college, and where both of them met. We have virtual dates over video calls, and I like her, I really do, but I worry about two weeks in that what's missing is her treating me like I'm disposable. I keep waiting to feel the burning twinge in the pit of my stomach when I talk to her, a feeling that was ever present around Moon-Hair Girl, and when I don't feel it, I think, *Well, was that feeling desire or fear, anyway?*

Multiple friends of mine assure me that it's *okay* to not have "butterflies" two weeks in, especially since this girl and I have yet to be in each other's physical presence. What I don't say in response to this, though, is that I once fell hard for a man I thought I loved who lived across the Atlantic Ocean and whose only communication with me was texts, audio messages, video calls, and snail mail letters. But if anyone knew how to treat me poorly while disguising it as love, it was him. You can see my confusion, I hope, with O., the girl who slings the scientific names of plants around and will eventually nickname me after one of her favorite tiny purple flowers.

At some point, I realize that my feelings for her become most apparent when I am forced to confront the possibility of her not being in my life, surely connecting to a looming fear of losing everything. Was it unfair to attach that weight to her? Probably, but I was grasping at straws, trying to keep my world from collapsing. In so many ways, so many of us were.

Near the end of April, when I am attempting to make plans to go back to Kansas for at least a short time, I am suddenly crying during therapy for a new reason, something besides the sadness and hurt I feel as a response to the pandemic:

"I know that nothing between us will actually change if I go back to Kansas, because we aren't able to see each other in person here," I say to my therapist through the screen of my computer, my voice doing the weird, hiccupping thing it does when I'm crying. "But things are going so well with O., and I don't want to lose that."

Then, O. cancels a date due to her own emotional warfare that day, and I find myself crying at the thought of not being able to see her that evening, not being able to comfort her, not being able to hug her. *So I like her,* I think. *I like her.*

but i cannot find the words

The question of when I will next return to school in Kansas is largely unanswerable, except for the fact that my next injection of Spinraza is due soon. The pandemic has caused the Interventional Radiology Department to enforce stricter policies for their patients—I will not be allowed, for example, to have anyone with me this time around.

My parents suggest making a phone call to see if there's any possibility that one of them can wear a mask and gloves, "suit up," and come back with me to the bay area where I wait to be wheeled into the operating room on a bed. If this isn't possible, a nurse will have to lift me from my wheelchair onto the bed, something that, although they are surely trained to do, is an action that varies from person to person. The idea of talking a nurse through exactly how to position my head and arms and legs exhausts me, and so I take my parents' advice and call, explaining the situation in a diplomatic yet convincing tone. Like battling insurance companies, this is an art I have mastered from twenty-five years of listening to my mom talk to any number of people who were in some way making decisions about what my life would look like: doctors, teachers, case managers. The woman I speak to in Interventional Radiology calls me back later that afternoon with good news: one person can come back with me.

The following day, I schedule my injection for June 1 and sit across from my helper in Des Moines while we both eat breakfast. We had made zucchini banana chocolate-chip muffins the night before, a recipe I'd been making since undergrad, one that usually provided me with breakfast, snacks, and dessert for well over a week.

"I was thinking about something the other night, and I want to tell you," I say, after taking a long drink of coffee through a straw. "If I get COVID, I don't want to go to the hospital."

"Okay," my helper says, matter-of-factly. Her mom has ovarian-cancer-turned-bladder-cancer, and my helper wants to be a hospice nurse. I'm thankful that I could tell her this difficult admission.

I'm not confident that a medical establishment largely unfamiliar with the specificities of different bodies, particularly bodies that look and function like mine, would be able to keep me alive. Up against COVID-19, it's possible that even people familiar with my body couldn't keep me alive—not a given, but not definitely possible. Without the people who know how to best care for me and the specific interventions someone with my disease does and doesn't need, it's hard for me to be hopeful. And more than anything, I do not want to die alone in a hospital.

It is perhaps worth mentioning that I always envisioned a different love interest being with me at an injection of Spinraza. Before I had made the decision to turn down Spinraza in Iowa, I imagined the man I thought I loved coming for my first injection. I always assumed my first sort-of girlfriend, A., would come with me, but our relationship didn't last long enough to mark the four-month dosing schedule. Moon-Hair Girl mentioned coming for one. And O., also, talked of one day coming. This is how much attraction and moments of physical vulnerability overlap in my mind, how much the thought of being alone during moments of physical vulnerability terrifies me.

Eight months in the future, after I have made it through pre-vaccine times while living at home with my parents, I will open Facebook to see a post from a woman around my age, also with SMA, leaving the hospital after a five-week stay, twenty-two days of which she was intubated due to COVID. *I was careful. I stayed away from people and places with risk, but the unimaginable still happened,* she had written, causing my stomach to clench. *In my thirty years of living with an underlying condition, this has by far been the hardest and scariest journey of my life.*

When I told the University of Iowa that they would not be drilling a hole in my spine to give me Spinraza, I did so in part because I could not make myself okay with the knowledge that I would have to be intubated for this, something which, because of the very specific risks associated with SMA and anesthesia, sometimes occurs prior to being put under, or with lighter sedation.

There is a Tweet, also, around this time that says how we need to be looking at COVID in more than the black-and-white *you will live, or you will die.* There is the in-between, in which you get COVID and don't die, but your life is forever and irrevocably changed. The Tweet is referring to long-haul symptoms, like those my chronically ill therapist is still dealing with six months after she recovered from COVID—pneumonia, brain fog, continued respiratory problems. But it's more than this, too: a study published in February 2021 will find that 30 percent of COVID survivors experience PTSD symptoms. For the woman I know with SMA who was hospitalized for five weeks due to COVID, and for so many others, surely there are psychological and emotional aftershocks of their experience. I don't know how there wouldn't be, just as I don't know how the physical, psychological, and emotional are not all intertwined.

While I'm brushing my teeth after breakfast that morning, my helper—who I had just told my wish to not go to the hospital if I were to catch COVID—asks me if I want to receive CPR if I suddenly stop breathing. "I mean, yeah," I say. I want to live.

"Okay," she says, again matter-of-factly. "The thing is, if you're resuscitated with CPR, you'll likely have to be taken to the hospital."

So, of course, nothing is really that simple.

I have a document on my computer called "If Shit Hits the Fan," which is my COVID-19 will and last wishes, for all intents and purposes.

I keep thinking of things I need to add (take, for example, not going to the hospital), but I cannot find the words.

DREAM

The Monster

You have a dream one night that you're looming over a being on a metal table, surrounded by doctors and nurses and onlookers, but you are the one holding the knife. The room is dark, like the room in the dream you have where a creature is being grown inside a vat of chemicals. In this dream, you feel an overpowering need to comfort the being on the table, although your comfort takes the form of poison, leaking out between your ~~fangs~~ teeth in a slippery, "Everything will be just fine," words that twist and flop and ooze and leave the stench of fear heavy in the air. You are drunk on the fact that for once, fear smells different because it is not your own.

MERMAID INTERLUDE

The Second Mermaid

You've heard about the king and his ludicrous outlawing of us, but do you understand why he did this? It's simple. So simple it's heartbreaking. The king couldn't stand the thought of women he couldn't fuck. He couldn't deal with it, couldn't fathom that we would give up the part of ourselves he (and, presumably, any other man) could enter. What he didn't understand is that it didn't matter to us; that in terms of pleasure, we knew other ways of getting the job done. For ourselves, for each other. Of course, we also knew how to pleasure men without what our tails took from us—this isn't the point because we largely didn't care.

The king was terrified of us because we were outside of what he could understand. "They must go at once," the formal proclamation read. "Our kingdom is not safe while mermaids live among us—they will seduce our sailors and lead them to their deaths." So you see, he taught them to fear us, and in doing so we became creatures who lived in fear. I wanted to tell the king that we had never actually killed anyone. That, it turns out, humans can make mistakes and crash their boats into outcrops of rocks and drown without half-humans luring them to do so.

The siren story is the one that got circulated, but it's not the truth. The truth is we hated being feared, and so, when we were able to, we moved as far away from humans as possible, but we still got a bad rep. Yes, we wailed. Yes, we cried. Yes, humans, particularly human males, found our crying beautiful. Do you know that human word, *schadenfreude*?

I refused to move away. To do so would have been to admit defeat—at least, this is what I allowed myself to believe, never seeing escape as its own revolution.

Instead, I lived for two years in a museum, pretending to be a sideshow attraction that was simply a shoddy illusion. The head and torso of a baby monkey sewn to the body of a giant catfish, emaciated and shrunken like a withered thief's hand.

This was a way for me to be protected, the oldest trick in the book: hiding in plain sight. Of course this came at a cost. Although I was safe, I had to endure the gasps of horror from children whose parents brought them to the museum as a way to kill time.

"What *is* that?" they would say, poking their fingers up against the glass of my case, knocking against it, refusing to hide their disgust because children aren't tamed, and so do not know how to hide their emotions. Their horror did not bother me because I knew, deep down, that what they were looking at was not actually me—the shriveled monkey head and catfish corpse was a trick of the light and a very skilled tattoo artist. Underneath the tattoos, I was just a normal enough looking woman, with an iridescent fish tail instead of legs. I knew this instinctively, and yet—

Each night, after the museum closed its doors and the last guard left for his home and wife and probably children (it's an old story, and in most of the old stories, the guards are men and the men have wives and children), I would release the metaphorical breath that I had been holding all day—the case I was in was arranged to hide the rise and fall of my breathing—and push through the back door of the case and let myself fall into the small pool of water attached to the back, housed in a back room of the museum. The silver of the pool's walls and the moonlight through the windows and the reflective nature of water . . . well, I saw myself mirrored back at me every night.

There was a woman I loved who was always writing, which was another reason I couldn't let myself leave—I couldn't bear the thought of exile without her. *The people on the page,* she told me once, *I created them and thus they are real.*

I'd let the tattoo artist spill ink into the layers of my skin so water couldn't wash off my disguise, and I'd taken the spot at the museum as a tattooed monkey fish so that I could stay alive and stay in the kingdom. *I created them and thus they are real.* What, then, had the tattoo artist created? I asked myself this each night, the question becoming more and more insistent until it drove me to keen and wail and pound my head against the sides of the pool, uttering strange animal noises, nothing like language, nothing like a human.

A guard found me in the morning like this, still in the pool, breathing heavily with blood dripping from a gash on my forehead. They closed the Hall of Oddities and tried to get me to speak. I grunted and moaned and grunted again.

What I wanted to say but had lost the words to: *you have created the monster before you.*

In Between the Staying and Going

The park behind my Iowa City apartment had picnic tables whose surfaces could easily be etched into and written on. My last summer living there, my helpers and I would leave messages on the wood on a weekly basis, sometimes in Sharpie, sometimes carved into the tabletop with a paperclip. The words were temporary, like the many chalked messages that would color the downtown sidewalks throughout the semester and summer: officially approved messages like *Dance Marathon meeting Tuesday #ForTheKids*, words scrawled under the cover of darkness like *Terrorists love the GOP*, and defiant exclamations of self, like that which my friend and helper Cole would write on the corner the morning of Iowa City's Pride: *Love from your favorite homo <3*.

While in undergrad, I took an essay workshop with Inara Verzemnieks, who had worked for eighteen years as a reporter before getting her MFA in Nonfiction Writing from the University of Iowa and then becoming an assistant professor. Inara believed heavily in details, and in the need for writers to become careful observers. On the first day of class, she gave each of us a notebook and instructed us to fill it with notes about a singular place by the end of February. I was a junior. I was studying Journalism and English myself. I thought I knew, then, the extent of my body's desires.

I took my reporter's notebook with me each week to The Mill, a bar and restaurant on Burlington Street that doubled as a music venue. When it got cold, I'd order the cheapest beer on the menu and drink in the afternoon in an attempt to warm myself up while I wrote about what was happening around me in the dark-green-tiled enclave with instruments hanging on the wall.

One night, a friend was performing in the back area of The Mill which turned into a stage, and I met E.—the source of my First Hurt and the burning in the pit of my stomach—there to watch.

E. and I met through my best friend, Haley, when a group of us got dinner together at Bluebird Diner, to this day my favorite Iowa City restaurant. A year or so later, E. and I were in a writing class together. She was a writer. I was a writer. We spent every Tuesday of one semester getting coffee together, and my body ached every time she mentioned her girlfriend. Later, she'd write a piece that described the shadows of a bonfire dancing on the shores of the Iowa River, a metaphor for nothing lasting.

After that night at The Mill, I wrote in my reporter's notebook that the darkness and the music and the headiness of the alcohol made me want to lean across the table into E.'s lips. I turned in the reporter's notebook, and even then, I thought nothing of the weight of what I had written. Later, I would sit in Inara's office, and she would recommend *The Argonauts* to me as a book written in a style she thinks I would like.

The Argonauts is the epitome of queer narratives. That summer, I'd listen as Maggie Nelson read her meandering love letter to her trans artist husband—dipping in and out of the second person—and something in the deep bloody marrow of my bones finally made sense.

But this is what I still keep returning to, years later. My hand held the pen which wrote the words *I wanted to lean over and kiss her* on the blue lines of a white page in a notebook that I would later give to my professor, and I *still* didn't consciously understand that I was attracted to women. What I'm trying to say is, I didn't have a wide enough space in my mind for my own understanding of my identity and sexuality. What I'm trying to say is, I didn't know what this space looked like because I never saw it. What I'm trying to say is, my body still knew.

Iowa City Pride was in its second, calmer shift. Cole and I wandered the streets that had been blocked off, dipping in and out of tents. Earlier that day I had changed out of my homemade rainbow Wonder Woman costume—a red and blue top, gold arm bands, rainbow sparkles on my face and a cardboard shield with the words "NEVERTHELESS SHE PERSISTED" painted across it—into shorts and a crop top, and the lessening of sparkle and pizazz in my outfit was reflected in the dispersed crowds and music which had morphed into a quieter, yet still energetic, soundtrack to our city's celebration.

Cole and I came across a free face painting booth, and I decided to get rainbow tears tattooed on my cheeks. "Have you had a good Pride?" the girl who was painting the rainbow drops on me asked. And while I could truthfully answer in the affirmative, I thought, also, of the goodbye on the horizon, and the unquenched longing the day had evoked in me.

Where are you? Sam texted me, shortly after my rainbow tears were complete.

Downtown and covered in glitter, I responded. *I'll head back to my place and meet you there.*

Cole and I walked back to my apartment and let Sam into the building, and I met Sam's gaze with a carefully crafted look of bubbly happiness.

I had eaten in front of Sam many times, had drank in front of him, had gotten out of my chair in front of him, had even let him take a photo of me while Cole washed my hair, although I had a towel wrapped around my body. The photo was for a project he was doing for our student newspaper, which we both worked for and was the reason we had become friends. He was writing a story about myself and Jenna, another, much younger girl with SMA, who was traveling to Iowa City to get injections of Spinraza, and who experienced spinal headaches frequently. The fact that I had agreed to Sam's story meant that a part of me trusted him, which was no small feat. As a journalism student surrounded by other journalism students who seemed to think "disability" was enough of a story topic to ask to write about me, I grew picky which stories I agreed to be a part of, what interviews I said yes to. *I can count on one hand the number of straight men that I trust,* I had once told my therapist. And Sam had made it to half a finger.

I was a year older than Sam, had been on the staff of the newspaper longer than him, and the first day I met him, he walked into the editors meeting and I swallowed my attraction to him deep down into the bottom of my feet, where I could keep it hidden until it disappeared. I was in the midst of a six-month, deeply unhealthy more-than-friendship with the man I thought I loved, and although the eventual combustion of this some-type-of-relationship broke me in ways I didn't even know I could be broken, it is the reason I could fit Sam into a *friends only* section of my mind, even after the semi-relationship was over.

When we got upstairs to my apartment, I told Sam I needed to get out of my chair, as I hadn't laid down all day. Cole lifted me onto my bed and got me situated on my side, and then sat in my wheelchair while Sam sat on the floor, his knees up in front of him. I don't know all that we talked about, but I assume it included the looming fact that we were both leaving. My intense love for Iowa City never made sense to Sam, who saw it as the proverbial party-littered college town (which, in so many ways, it was).

At some point, we started talking about my search to find helpers in Kansas, where I would be moving in two months. "Do you think you'll hire more male helpers?" Sam asked.

"I might, but I likely would never hire a straight male. I don't think I would trust them." The words I left unspoken were that people with disabilities are sexually abused at a rate twice as high as non-disabled individuals, and that perpetrators of abuse were largely people in their life—for instance, caregivers.

"You'd trust me though, wouldn't you?" Sam responded.

I didn't respond right away. "Yeah," I finally said. "I mean, maybe." I made a joke then about Sam's general lateness to events and unreliability and skirted around an explanation of the *maybe*. There was a part of me, even then, that hated how little I seemed to be able to trust straight men and was hopelessly confused about this part of myself.

"You know, Hannah," Cole said, "you don't have to justify who you want as your helpers. You deserve to hire the people you're comfortable hiring, and you don't have to explain that."

Cole was right.

Eventually Sam would get up to leave and come over to hug me good-bye. I rarely let straight men touch me. To feel fully comfortable in this hug from him meant that the moment he walked out my apartment door I broke into tears—at the fact that this friendship would have to change due to both of our moving, at the fact that I was leaving these people and this city, where I had discovered my independence, at the fact that I *wanted* to be able to tell Sam I would trust him, but couldn't.

Also in Iowa City: the cat I would eventually bring home from the shelter, the cat we would let out in the bathtub because he had shit in the cardboard carrier the shelter gave me to take him home in, the cat who would cry incessantly for three nights in a row, surely not knowing what to make of his new surroundings.

He was a street cat, the shelter told me. Which is, they reasoned, how he had contracted FIV (like HIV, but for felines). When I breezed into the shelter on the day I would get to bring him home, the woman who helped check me out said, "Oh! You're getting the hugger!" Which, it would turn out, I was. Every time a shelter staff opened his cage to feed him or change his litter box, he would stretch up to place his front paws on their shoulders, around their neck.

This was an endearing trait my helpers and I would love him for, the cat I had decided to name Mercury, after the messenger of the gods. And what I would love Mercury for even more, more than his purrs and his antics and his eyes like deep pools of liquid, was the time, right near the beginning, when he climbed all over my desk and lap in the midst of me FaceTiming the man I thought I loved, putting his body between me and the man's face. *I will protect you,* he seemed to say in his glance back at me, in the twitch of his ears. *I will protect you because there is something here to be protected from, even if—and this is important—it's the eventual breaking of your own heart.*

The beginning of the saga with the man I thought I loved took place through a Facebook message, my phone buzzing as I sat in the froyo shop downtown in Iowa City, with Haley and a few other friends. It ended with Haley and I burning all the letters he had sent me, outside in the dead of winter, in the parking lot behind my apartment.

Please understand, I grew up not believing men would be attracted to me, that I was a novelty to be used and conquered. You will forgive me, then, for cutting myself open for a man with a fiery soul and crooked smile who showed me the slightest interest. And you will forgive me, also, for being broken by his inability to match my expectations.

I would have to tell Haley goodbye in this same parking lot, each of us crying by her car as she hugged me tight, mere days before I moved from Iowa City. I was terrified of everything changing. I knew that change was undeniable.

In the fall of my first year of graduate school, where I was trying and trying, and failing and failing, to leave my years in Iowa behind me, a friend and I make cookie dough edibles one night at my apartment and get appallingly stoned, me to the point of a panic attack I thought would never end. After my friend had caught an Uber back to her apartment and I had told my helper to just put me in bed, no pajamas, no brushing my teeth, no washing my face, I lay on my side in the dark and stared at the designs being painted on the insides of my eyelids. A tiny, sober, and buried part of me knew that I just had to wait this out, as I had waited out bad trips in the past. I just had to lull myself into sleep, and when I returned to consciousness the following morning everything would have righted itself, the world around me would stop spinning, and I would know what to do.

But as the colorful triangles that had taken up residence in front of my vision continued to shimmer and dance, the same thought kept thrumming itself through my mind: *I am still attracted to him, and oh, how I am attracted to her.* Him, of course, being Sam, whose friendship I had worked to maintain over the past year of us living in different states and who I had convinced myself I saw in just that careful category, that exact definition: friend. Sam was unattainable, and thus safe. Is this why I could still be attracted to him? She was less unattainable, less safe. Was this also why I was attracted to her? She was the one my helper and I had just helped get into an Uber, who I had already decided I would turn myself inside out for.

I would wake up the next morning, and I would, of course, not know what to do. But those two truths—my two attractions—shone with a brightness I could not ignore.

That heat-soaked summer, I would come home from a date with a softly handsome man (a date I had to drink bourbon mixed with lemon to get through, not because he was awkward or uncomfortable, but because this was the only way, I learned, I could mask my anxiety of being around straight men) to encounter the flooding realization that I have no desire, ever, to be physically intimate with men, and that my anxiety surrounding romance and intimacy with men is there because physical intimacy with men is something I have no wish for in my life.

At the end of the date, the man asked if he could hug me, and because I was sated with alcohol, I had said yes.

"You're a good hugger," I told him. It wasn't a lie. But it didn't mean I could fully feel myself relaxing into the weight of his hands on my back. We had met through a mutual friend, and when we briefly talked about her before I started in on my drink, I wondered, from the way I carefully measured my words, if he could tell it was her I was actually into.

I had grown up not believing men could be attracted to me, and yet here in front of me was proof that they could. Here, across the bar's table, separated by our drinks and a candle, was an attractive man, a nice man, a charming man, who lightly touched my wrist, who remarked on the brightness of my eyes, who wanted to find a way for me to come to his inaccessible house. It was everything I thought I had ever wanted, and everything I thought I would never get. And now that it was possible, within reaching distance, I realized I didn't want it.

Back at my apartment, as my helper was bringing me my toothbrush, I spoke aloud the words I now knew to be true. "I think I'm gay."

"Probably," she said, and we laughed and laughed and laughed, and I felt, suddenly, my reality click into place and a lightness wash through me. But then I started crying, because why had it taken me this long (twenty-three years) to figure this out? Why had I let myself be shaped so much by how I perceived others perceiving me? And what had I been missing out on, trying to date men? I was suddenly so sad, and so angry at the world and circumstances which had led me to shy away from my own exploration of my sexuality and romance as a disabled woman.

The next day, I went on my second date with the girl who would become my first, if short-lived, loosely defined girlfriend. We had decided to meet on the rooftop of the Oread, a weird, landmark hotel that sat at the top of a hill and whose patio roof allowed us to look down over the city. When I told her my realization, she hugged me and then told me that it was okay if there came a time later in my life where I was attracted to men, or wanted to be intimate with men, or wanted to date men, and that I could still be a lesbian. At the time, as the evening winds whipped through both of our hair, this muddled definition of attraction and sexuality didn't make sense to me. But I've come to understand a certain truth—that a label is an estimate of meaning, at best. Categories can only hold so much. I had spent years subconsciously burying my attraction to women, this integral and special part of my being. I hope to never turn around and do the same thing with a potential attraction to men, just because of the assumed boundaries of a word.

And still, another truth:

Sometimes I wonder if my identifying as gay is subconsciously only a way for me to make sense of the brokenness I acquired from the man I thought I loved, who loved how the meanings of words could change. As in, am I truly only attracted to women, or is this identity formation simply a way for the me that is me before any sort of performance of me to make sense of the past pain? As a writer, I weave people into narratives and sometimes these people take on meaning beyond just themselves: they become person as signifier. If this man became symbolic of a container which I believed could hold my soul, what does the eventual breaking of us mean?

The first time I had let Sam hug me was in an empty room of the journalism building on campus, after I had asked him to come with me to retrieve a threatening and explicit letter that had been addressed to me and sent to the place I used to work. My old boss, who worked in the journalism building, had gotten it and alerted me, as its return address was a prison in Texas. Months prior, I had published a piece of writing on disability and sexuality in a highly visible national magazine, and the writer of the letter—who was in prison for child molestation convictions—had read it, decided they wanted to send me a sexually explicit letter asking me to be theirs, and found the address to do so through my LinkedIn.

"I don't know what to do," I cried in the empty classroom, my helper and friend rubbing my back and Sam leaning against a desk, his hands on his knees. "That piece was really vulnerable and open. Should I just not write that type of stuff anymore?"

"You're absolutely not going to stop writing that stuff," Sam said. "You're going to keep writing vulnerable and open work, and we're going to get this figured out."

"Okay," I said. *Okay.*

"Can I hug you?" he asked, and for a fraction of a moment I could feel myself relaxing into his hug.

Later, I went to the Iowa City Police Station to file a report at the suggestion of Fi, now in law school, and be greeted by five steps up to the door through which I'd need to enter if I wanted a private room to explain to an officer what had happened. Later, after leaving the police station and still not knowing what to do, I would answer the phone to hear the voice of one of my favorite writers on the other end, telling me I had gotten into the MFA program where she teaches, and that she was hoping I would accept. I had already accepted my position in Kansas, where the financial aid package was much better, and because I was still reeling from the letter, I was short with her, telling her I had already made my decision. My brusqueness on the phone that day is something I still think about and regret. And later—Sam and I would set fire to the letter behind my apartment, watching the words curl and vanish into nothing.

Hunger

I've been devoting all of my energy to finding other things to fill my mind besides the face and the voice of the girl I met at a coffee shop and then a park and then a restaurant, and the way the black inked her skin and the moon turned the edge of her hair on fire. As I lay on the tattoo bench and bare my shoulder to the ink and needle, I keep thinking of her, Moon-Hair Girl above me instead of this man, her smirk and her dark eyes, similar, in a way, to the smirk and the eyes of the man I once thought I loved. *You've got to get her out of her head, Hannah,* I keep thinking, the hum of the tattoo needle in the background. *You've got to get her out of her head.*

I'm back in Kansas after spending Thanksgiving at home in Iowa. The tattoo artist I am paying to carve into the skin of my collarbone keeps getting up from his work to make sure my wheelchair is still secure at the bottom of the steps. The door we came in through locks, he assures my helper and I, but still, periodically, he checks. Before getting comfortable on the bench and pulling my shirt down past my shoulder, I had my helper carry me up a flight of stairs to the tattoo shop. This is a key detail I hide from my parents until later, the fact that the tattoo shop I am going to is only accessible by a long, narrow staircase, and that I am trusting my helper to cradle my body all the way up.

I'm getting a wolf—a wolf crouched and stretching out its front paws and nearly smiling, a wolf that is *cute*, as the tattoo artist says. Any further background on the tattoo is not important. What's important is that the pain of the needle is weirdly relaxing, and I find myself closing my eyes and letting myself sink into the experience. This is tattoo number fourteen, and I haven't experienced one quite like this yet. At one point, with Ben Howard's *Old Pine* playing in the background, I think I am going to drift into a comfortable sleep.

Roxane Gay has written about her relationship with getting tattoos, and how they are a way for her to exercise control over her body. For me, it's this and more: a subconscious way for me to attempt to integrate this bodily pain into a pleasurable experience. If I can overwrite this bodily pain with a sense of pleasure because I chose it, perhaps I can make the experience of getting Spinraza injected into my spinal fluid with a needle every four months less traumatic. I am choosing to have that procedure, but I am not choosing the pain, or the circumstances under which the procedure is done. The pain of the tattoo, the design of the tattoo, the tattoo artist—all this I have control over, all this I choose.

Later that spring, I have a doctor's appointment with my neurologist, who is overseeing the spinal injections. I have somehow lost ten pounds, quite a bit for someone as small as I am, someone with as little muscle as I have. It is suggested by my doctors that the ten pounds probably needs to be gained back, and I try to do this, except it seems like the ten pounds was probably lost due to stress and I haven't quite figured out how not to be stressed. I try eating more, but even when I eat more, I'll be hungry within an hour. I don't know how else to eat. What sort of body is this?

I know the warning story of the woman with my disease who didn't eat anything except bites of ice cream for three days after her boyfriend broke up with her and ended up in the hospital, her organs shutting down because her body, in an attempt to feed itself, had turned to her muscles, which she didn't have, and so had gone for her organs. I know from this to eat at least three meals a day, even when anxiety has shut down my appetite. It's almost a reversal, then—this insatiable hunger that I can't seem to satisfy, that still is leaving my body smaller and smaller. In the warning story, I don't know why I separate *the body* and *her*. I don't say "it turned to its muscles," or "she turned to her muscles"—

do human pronouns signify conscious thought? What do I mean by that, anyway—human pronouns?

My cousin Sarah, in school for environmental science and always armed with facts about (supposedly) non-human creatures, tells me a story one night about spiders that keep rebuilding their webs each morning after they'd been destroyed by the storm the night before. When she tells me this, my mind flashes immediately to the spider that lived on our picnic table one summer after I'd fallen for a girl in my writing class, the first girl I consciously had feelings for. That spider, these spiders, their resilience makes me inward-howl—a keening that no one can hear. Sarah tells me that the woman studying these spiders would remove parts of their webs and replicate them with floss and then replace them in the exact spot she had stolen them from. The spiders would tear them down and start over. Is this resilience, or stubbornness, or simply being trapped? If resilience is a trait that some of us have sharpened in order to survive, in these situations, do we have any other choice?

Do the spiders have a choice? Couldn't they just move to a safer spot to spin their web? Couldn't they?

I buy a slow feeder bowl for my cat. His overzealousness toward food resulted in vomiting up his undigested kibble directly after scarfing it down. A glistening drop of blood on his chin from a scratch sends my stomach into a network of knots because I think, in some small, terrified corner of my mind, that I have failed him. I think, after I have bought this flat orange dish that looks like a waffle with different compartments for the food and he is still throwing up, that my attempts to get him to eat normally is only an outward manifestation of the anxiety I have toward my own uncontrollable body.

"How's your appetite?" my mom asks me. This comes after a twenty-five-minute phone conversation in which I gulped out my sadness over the girl I'd been talking to for the past three months, the girl whose hair turned to fire under the light of the moon, not wanting to actually date.

I still wanted the feel of her skin between my teeth but didn't know how to share this with my mom.

"Weirdly good," I said. Which was true: I didn't feel like I had to force myself to eat, I was still hungry, my stomach—although certainly still a holding cell for my anxiety—seemed to be cooperating. I wondered if this was because the anxiety that usually transformed the pit of my stomach to a barbed-wire minefield had been overtaken by pure sadness. I didn't want to be in Kansas. I didn't want to be in the grad program I was in. I didn't want to not be with her.

Still, I go to bed hungry that night, and I wouldn't be telling the absolute unfiltered truth if I said the small ache of not being full wasn't in some way comforting. After the first girl I fell for, I spent nights without sleep from the pins in my stomach and vowed to never go to bed hungry again (because, after all, this is what I attributed the pain to—a lack of food before bed, not heartbreak). Now, the physical pain of heartbreak is something familiar.

The night before I have a wolf etched into my collarbone, my parents and I are eating enchiladas in my Lawrence apartment after they've driven me back to Kansas after Thanksgiving break. We're talking about the time I left Iowa City, where I lived for five years while getting my bachelor's, and all the clearing out I had done before moving. I'd had an autograph of Misha Collins, an actor I was obsessed with, on the plastic overlay of a photo of his arm around my shoulders, both of us smiling goofily. When I left Iowa City, I had tossed this all into the trash without a care.

"You've always been good at letting things go," my mom said.

"I suppose, yes." *Except for people*, I thought. "Except for people. I'm bad at letting go of people."

My mom tells me this is good, that holding people close is a strength, not a weakness, but I don't know if this is true. Is it bad to not be able to let go of the people who are hurting you? What if they are not actively hurting you, but staying in their presence is hurting you just the same? What I mean is, in the words of Jenny Boully, "why is it that I have feet and yet still refuse to flee?"

Reasons to stay: the electric shock from the back of your neck to the base of your spine every time she says your name, the other people in your life aren't like her, he tells you you're beautiful just like the stars, you've learned to call this place home.

Reasons to leave: the electric shock from the back of your neck to the base of your spine every time she says your name, the other people in your life aren't like her, he tells you you're beautiful just like the stars, you've learned to call this place home.

If trauma entails leaving, i.e. if the processing of trauma entails being able to leave the place of trauma unscathed, i.e. if trauma is inherently tied to place, at what point is it time to leave, and at what point is it better to stay? If we measure distance in days since we've spoken, what length is enough?

The girl with the moon-hair, understand, is not just Moon-Hair Girl, but an accumulation of past individuals who have made me stumble and gasp and fall on my knees. "Fall on my knees" is of course a metaphor, as my body cannot follow the paths carved out by this language. Some disability studies scholars would say that this very phrase carries an indication of value, specifically on those bodies which can follow those paths. But in my mind, that is what I am doing—falling on my knees, curling around my center, reaching out my arms to the feet of the people who have left me.

I will send Moon-Hair Girl songs by Brandi Carlile, as I will send Brandi Carlile songs to nearly every girl I wish to turn myself inside out for. If someone tells me they do not like Brandi Carlile's music, I will remember the way tears spilled out of my eyes under the Kansas sunset as she told the outdoor amphitheater about her wife and daughters, and how she believes it's important to stand in front of her audiences and tell them about her family because they are her family and have as much right to be her family as anyone else.

I will send Moon-Hair Girl "Save Part of Yourself" and "Wherever Is Your Heart" and, perhaps out of a subconscious need for irony, "Touching the Ground," which points to heartache wherever someone's feet meet the ground. Palms touching palms, soles touching earth. Hunger leaving me empty.

How do we express pain through language if we don't have the language to do so? What I mean is, how do I write about my body without slipping into somebody else's skin?

The last time I saw her before it ended, the girl I had been talking to, the girl who didn't want to date, the girl with hair that blazed under the moonlight drove my wheelchair-accessible van and strapped me into my wheelchair and helped me position my food and water within reaching distance. When her tom yum soup came first, she offered me a mushroom with her spoon, which I desperately wanted to take but knew I could not manipulate into my mouth with the spoon they had given her.

Later, after she had taken me back to my house and I had given her a tour and we had stalled and stalled and stalled some more and she had finally told me I was sleepy and she would leave so I could go to bed, I told my parents I didn't know what to do because she was still so shy in my eyes, still a tough one to crack. *Well, she's probably never done anything like that before*, my mom had said. *Did you eat anything?* Yes, I had. That was a first—eating in front of someone I was so desperately attracted to. Even in my last actual relationship, I never ate in front of the girl I was dating. Later, a whole six months later, when she and I had ended things but were still very good friends, I finally ate a lemon bar in front of her because I was hungry and didn't want to leave the coffee shop early just so I could go home and eat.

Please understand, this is not a narrative of an eating disorder or an unhealthy relationship with food—this is a narrative of an unhealthy relationship, at least to some degree, with my body.

This girl, van-driving girl, tom yum soup girl, had gotten a straw for me and bent my spoon for me so I could eat the rice in my mango stir fry without it spilling everywhere, and yes, mom, I had eaten, I had eaten, I had eaten, but no, it was not enough and yes, I was still hungry.

My body acts out in reaction to romantic relationships not working out. I threw up each morning for a week following the end of an incredibly tumultuous friend-but-more-than-friendship with the first person I truly thought I loved. Realizing that tom yum soup girl and I would never date caused me to cry for hours on end, days in a row. What broke me then might have not broken someone else. Why does my body do this?

Like the recurring dream I had in which my fingers were bandaged due to multiple cuts I had willingly endured, pain is not always commensurate with the injury. My hands in this dream always seared in agony, but the cuts were tiny and shallow (though bloody, nonetheless)—no tearing of ligaments, no breaking of bones. There's an illustration I came across once that showed a full-grown wolf standing over a baby wolf, the baby wolf bleeding out from a single arrow in its back. The adult wolf has been shot three times but is still living.

I once listened to an interview with writer Junot Diaz in which he said that love is especially painful for those who have not had positive representations of their communities engaged in romantic relationships. I have no memory of the first media representation that I saw of a romantic relationship involving a disabled individual, although it might have been *Me Before You*, which ends in suicide. Junot Diaz's theory, then, applies perfectly to the disability community (and to some extent, also, the queer community)—that this extra level of pain comes from an insatiable hunger for something that we do not see reflected to us in the stories that are told.

For the man I thought I loved (and this is important to the story because this is important to the truth), I made myself into someone he wanted, which was also a version of myself I wanted to become. I pretended confidence and experience and worked hard to exude sex appeal—somewhat of a fake it 'til you make it, yes, but here is the kicker, the pain that lingers: part of what broke me was feeling that he had taken advantage of my youngness and naivete, which I sweated to hide. I wouldn't be giving him enough credit if I said he was completely unaware of this, of what he was doing, but I was a co-author of that story, too. Maybe we both twisted truths, maybe we both hurt each other.

This man penned letters to me, letters that described the four types of love, the modes in which he saw the world, the colors that came to him when he spoke my name. *He makes me a better person,* I said to my best friend Haley one night over the phone. At this point it is perhaps obvious that I had come to equate *better* with *confused.*

Moon-Hair Girl is one of those people who pulls a longing from the back of my throat every time she texts me. Her name lights up on my phone screen, and I feel tears welling in the back of my eyes because I know that my longing for her doesn't make sense, because of what I know she cannot give me.

Sometimes to a fault, I imagine what others are thinking. With Moon-Hair Girl, I need to know what iteration of "disabled" I am in her mind. Or am I any? There are drawbacks to becoming aware of how your people have been theorized about, even if there is still something liberatory about absorbing, for the first time, stories you have lived.

Rosemarie Garland-Thomson cites the disabled figure as one that is constructed, and one that functions as "a synecdoche for all forms that culture deems non-normative." Like the time I saw myself in the floor-length dance studio mirror and was struck with my bodily difference, I know that my body doesn't "make sense," that it is *deemed* to not make sense.

There is something to be said about the ability to hold two contradictory truths at the same time—I want to do this often, especially in regard to the relationship I have with my body: *I want to be able to raise my hand to her face/I don't want to be cured.* But this somehow feels very different from *I like you/I don't want to be with you.*

I realize in retrospect that I have come quite a way since what I consider to be the First Hurt, in which I assumed a girl's heavy flirtations with me meant she wanted to be with me. Things, I have found, are never that straightforward. "Hannah, that's just how she is, incredibly flirtatious,"

Haley had told me of the girl I had met through her and who had awoken something within me that I did not know existed. The man I thought I loved embodied the contradictory in many ways: *I will love you/I will hurt you*; *I want you/I want her more.*

Do you need to learn to stay in order to know how to leave? I don't know how to stop writing about heartbreak (*heartbreak*, of course, being a contentious word, as there is no apparent physical injury).

The clawing feeling in the pit of my stomach is one that I have run from for so long, while at the same time, ran toward. At some point after she leaves, I realize that when I eat, I am always thinking about how much I will need to eat to feel full, and how long that will hold me over until I am hungry again.

DREAM

The Masochist

You have a dream one night that you are defending the girl who pulls longing from the back of your throat to a roomful of people who are saying she will eat you alive. You finally have to leave because you can't stomach hearing the things they are saying about her, things you know to be true. There's always a pool in your dreams, or at least more often than not. And this pool materializes as you are leaving the room, through the doorway it appears as a shimmering hole in the floor, filled with water. Between the edges of the pool and the wall closest to you is a space as narrow as the reality you have defined for yourself. Of course she is sitting on the other side of the pool. The way the sunlight through the window burns the edges of her hair makes your stomach clench. *Well*, she said, *go around the pool. You know you have to, it's the only way.* What you fail to realize is that you don't have to, that there is another way. To get to her, yes, certain death is the only way. But reaching her is never the only option. Dream-you somehow balances on the edge of the pool and inches along, until suddenly your body splits in half, and part of you sinks beneath the water.

MERMAID INTERLUDE

The Third Mermaid

The story is simple, and because it's so simple, it's all the more heartbreaking.

We were sitting in my living room, him on the couch and me in the bathtub we had dragged out from the bathroom after the unfortunate morning in which I had woken up with a tail. The water was tepid, which I was getting used to. The king had already announced his plan to rid the land of mermaids, but given it was the middle of the night, we had the windows open, letting in the moonlight. He looked so beautiful sitting there, the light from the fire—its warmth didn't quite reach me—casting intoxicating shadows over his face. The eyes of my cat gleamed from the corner where he sat, always watching.

"We were both drunk, and I looked over at her and suddenly had this moment of clarity," he said. He was talking to me about the woman he pined for, another reality I was getting used to. His eyes smoldered. The fire smoldered.

He continued: "'I should kiss you, right?' I asked her, and she just smiled and leaned into me, and it was like I was tasting the finest wine for the first time in my life. And she read to me after, lines from her own work interspersed with Joyce." He sighed. "It was bliss. Her body and her voice and her words were bliss."

I swallowed the urge to roll my eyes.

He was one of those disgustingly eloquent poet types. Everything had to be a goddamn metaphor to him, for which I would always hate him and love him in equal measures. We had been thrown together by chance years and years and years ago, and I kept my desire for him hidden behind tales of kissing women, just as the tail I'd woken up with one morning hid my no-longer-working legs.

He worked as a guard at the museum, a job he said was wasted on him. That is, until the morning of the Hall of Oddities incident, a scene he stumbled upon before the other guards (who had, in fact, gone home to their wives and children, unlike the man in my living room, who did not have a wife, just a mermaid and a woman who read him Joyce). He described in detail the way he found the mermaid bleeding and incoherent, raging one minute, mournful the next. "A perfect symbol for our failures as humans," he had told me that night. "She's the most beautiful monster." I winced. He tried to take back his words. "You . . . you know I don't think of *you* as a monster, right?" I knew he didn't. That is, I knew he believed he didn't.

I left him, gradually. Or he left me. Some things could never survive the king's plan.

The Way the Clock Bends to Our Bodies

OCTOBER 20XX

Before I get vaccinated and move back to Kansas, I sit in my childhood bedroom and make a post-pandemic bucket list with Sierra, a helper who gets tested and comes to Iowa for a week each month during the duration of the first fall and winter of COVID-19.

On the list:

Host a fancy champagne party.

See Harry Styles in concert.

Go to all the lesbian bars in Chicago.

Eventually, I realize I have a nearly unbreakable habit of beginning sentences with clauses that indicate time.

Back in Kansas, I slowly delete the words "post-pandemic" from the designated note in my phone and replace it with "Vaxxed in Kansas Summer." The items on the list change too. *Post*, of course, implies an after, and *after* implies an ending, something I no longer believe in.

Feminism and disability studies scholar Alison Kafer discusses the "role of disability in imagined futures," and argues that within the context of the medical complex—that is, within the context of a cure—disability is seen as an "obstacle" to the "arc of progress," disabled people as people "out of time." "Out of time" as in "time's up"? Or "out of time" as in "outside of this thing we use to make sense of our world"? I don't know. Maybe both, maybe neither.

As my mom drives me back to Kansas, I use the mile markers on the side of the road to tick off distance, simple calculations performed in my head to estimate time. Things are safer now, where I'm heading. But you can still drive over backroad bridges and see trees ripped from the ground and laid in circular patterns where the tornadoes touched down.

July 20xx

When I lay in bed with the first girl I kissed, I lay there with my heart beating to the knowledge that we were both in that shared space on borrowed time. She had the busiest social life of anyone I have yet to meet, and our somehow chaste make-out sessions always ended with her reaching up to the head of my bed where she'd put her phone to check the hour, the minute.

It would have been easy for me to internalize this and believe I wasn't worth more of her time, but somehow our eventual ending wasn't fueled by a hurt, and I visualized her leaving each date as a harried yet vibrant wanderer who was always chasing after a figure of a clock.

Years later, I lay in bed with hook-ups and ask them what time it was, always wanting to make sure we had enough time before they had to leave, or before my next helper would arrive.

Not related to physical intimacy—I nearly always know the approximate time when asked without having to look at a clock because of how ingrained time has become in my day. I have to keep myself from glancing at the clock in the upper right-hand corner of my laptop when I'm working, so I changed it to analog instead of digital so I could not obsessively watch the minutes tick by. I get antsy when I'm behind schedule by a few minutes because I know the amount of minutes it takes me to do daily things.

In Ireland, when a group of other students in the program were complaining about the workload of our classes, I went back to my dorm room to lay down, had my helper open the window to fresh Irish air, and thought to myself, *We all have the same twenty-four hours in the day. This work doesn't feel like a lot to me because my survival has depended upon knowing how to work with time.* I was only right about one of these statements—how I've learned to work with time—although this inaccuracy of the first statement is largely contingent upon your definition of "the same." We may all be operating under the same human-constructed timetable, but that doesn't mean our experiences of time are equal. The woman working four minimum wage jobs to pay her bills and buy groceries for herself and her children does not have the same twenty-four hours in a day as the woman who is able to sustain herself on a part-time job, due to generational wealth, family support, a partner that works, etc. They each have twenty-four hours in a day, but how those hours are devoured by their needs differ.

The factors which play into this are endless—it takes me two to three times longer than my non-disabled peers to both get ready in the morning and at night. Likewise, panic attacks and deep depressive states suck up time. My friend and fellow SMA-er Brooklyn once told me, "I swear, I spend half the day being disabled, and the other half I just want to rest," and I thought, *Yes, that's it.* This is the same reason I could never bring myself to go out and party till the wee hours of the morning like my non-disabled college friends, and why I'm still hesitant to be out late at night: when non-disabled peers get home from a night out, they can get ready for bed and be asleep in fifteen minutes; for me, the process takes at least an hour and a half. Of course, the fifteen minutes between getting home and bed is only a reality to some, disability or no. If you're a single parent putting your kids to bed, for example, your understanding and measurement of this time may be quite different.

Lorin, the helper and friend I was with the night I realized I was gay (an approximate meaning), used to tell me how impatient I was, tied as I was pre-pandemic to the clock. She was always partially joking, a friendly roast steeped in truth.

"I'm not impatient," I would tell her. "I have a different relationship with time because of how I've always had helpers coming in and out of my days, and it takes me longer to do things so I know when I need to start things and when I need to be done with them."

Because I have had a rotating team of roughly anywhere from nine to thirteen people helping me with all my daily living activities for the past eight years, and because some of these shifts are three hours and some of them are twelve, and because it takes some helpers longer to do certain tasks than others, and because certain things take me longer to do because my muscles move slow, and ok, yes, because I like having control over that which I can control, I have gotten quite skilled at counting the time.

In response to my monologue on how I courted the clock, Lorin would always say, "I know, and I understand that, but you're still impatient."

Her comment only slightly bothered me because I only slightly believed that my understanding and relationship with time was something I could translate to others. And if it wasn't something I could make clear to those who did not dance the devil's dance with time, then I was okay with being thought of as a little bit impatient. As a present, once, Lorin gave me a pin in the shape of the impatiens flower, which I proudly had her put on my backpack.

What I would learn, eventually, is that she was right. The devil's dance with time was such for a reason. My needs take time, yes, but I don't have to view this need as devouring. There came a stage of the pandemic where I moved beyond imagining how I would accomplish everything I'd ever wanted to in all this spare time, and could now see the next minutes, the next hours, the next days stretch out in front of me like sea waves and then dry up into oblivion with a snap and a blink. The numbers that made up how we control time stopped making sense to me, stopped bleeding me dry.

June 20XX

The letters SMA stand for Spinal Muscular Atrophy, but only within certain contexts. At camp as a kid, my friends and I made up other meanings of the acronyms of our conditions—CMT didn't mean Charcot-Marie-Tooth, it meant Country Music Television, and SMA became Salsa Music Association. M, apparently, could never mean anything besides music.

I went to camp for the first time when I was ten. Prior to this, SMA meant Spinal Muscular Atrophy, but also something else—So Many Angels. My family and I had been heavily involved in the organization Families of SMA since I was diagnosed, and for a while in those early years of its being, the group had a logo that looked like an angel made out of the letters SMA, with the phrase *So Many Angels* beneath it. I would have seen this image over and over as a child—no wonder I expected to not live past adolescence, like the late disability rights lawyer and writer Harriet McBryde Johnson, whose book *Too Late to Die Young* I would first encounter during my freshman year of college. Her book opens with a scene of her watching a commercial for the Muscular Dystrophy Association as a child in the early sixties and realizing that she is the same as the child in the commercial. She has a disease similar to his. He died. Therefore, she will die young, too. She starts to refer to her awareness of mortality as the coffin in the basement.

Harriet McBryde Johnson was an instrumental figure in the protests surrounding the MDA's early messaging around Muscular Dystrophy as a tragedy and death sentence. But with Families of SMA, it's too simple of a conclusion to make, that phrases like So Many Angels should never have occurred. Because at least for a time, SMA was the number one killer of children under the age of two, another fact I heard frequently growing up. It is still the leading genetic cause of death for infants, a slight tweaking of language that is, at least for me, unclear in its meaning. Regardless, there *were* so many angels, and the fact that there are now perhaps *fewer* angels of babies and kids with SMA is due, in part, to advancements in treatments and medicine, which were, in part, lobbied for and funded by Families of SMA, no longer So Many Angels.

In 2014, Families of SMA changed their name to CureSMA, a change that brought about much outrage by some SMA-ers and their family members. Defenders of the name change, including adults with SMA who had been instrumental in the decision to change the title, said that this would allow for more funding to be acquired through grants. This is not a sentence about which name I prefer, simply a sentence about how each name carves out different shapes and holds different meanings—*families* implies connection and togetherness, perhaps even a glimmer of a future as the branches of family trees reach up and out; *cure* implies a strict arc of progress, straightforward and unbending.

April 20XX

I first saw Kara Walker's art the summer after my freshman year of high school in New York at the Museum of Modern Art. Her piece *Gone: An Historical Romance of a Civil War as It Occurred b'tween the Dusky*

Thighs of One Young Negress and Her Heart sprawls fifty feet wide across one wall. The helper who was with me took a photo of the entire piece on her camera, and we zoomed in on all the sections of it later, back where we were staying. For the rest of that trip and years afterward, I could not get this piece out of my mind.

Walker is a contemporary Black artist who works in silhouettes. She cuts life-size (and sometimes larger than life) outlines out of black paper. From a distance, her pieces appear whimsical. She features many girls and young women in acts of (apparent) play, many set outdoors. The scene she has painted looks a bit like a Black Neverland, magical and fun. But up close, Walker's art takes on a much more horrific hue—the little girl in braids who you think is dancing is actually dropping babies from between her legs; the woman under the tree leaning in to kiss the man doesn't see his sword drawn behind his back, just as he doesn't notice her extra pair of child-like legs protruding from her dress, an anomaly mirrored in the woman holding a broom, atop a masculine form in a tailcoat whose head seems to have entered her body from below. She spits something from her mouth in shock, and it is frozen in its descent to the ground. This is the violent Antebellum south put into a storybook-like narrative.

In high school, inspired by Walker, I created my own silhouette mural out of black and white paper. Unlike Walker, I could not cut giant shapes from paper myself, so I drew the scenes on paper before transferring them to the clear plastic sheets that were used on projector machines. This was before Smart boards became a standard item in classrooms, and Elmo projectors (also called "ladybugs") were just becoming common.

"I've worked with Kara Walker before!" my art teacher Mr. Weiss (who we simply called Weiss) told me. "She's incredible."

Weiss was always so much more than simply our high school art teacher. He hosted "lunch club," where students, including the boy I had a desperate crush on, would eat lunch in the art room instead of the cafeteria and laugh over Weiss's antics. He was in design classes with my mom in college. He had been teaching so long at our high school that my one-on-one helper through the school, Katie, who had also attended high school there, had him as her art teacher as well. He loved birds—

would photograph dead ones he found—and so we affectionately called the gray curls on top of his head a bird's nest. Weiss's proximity to my favorite artist at that time made me love Kara Walker even more.

After I finalized my drawings of the scenes, Katie and I found an empty dressing room connected to the stage where we could project my drawings onto the wall and trace them onto huge swaths of black paper. Then, with the assistance of friends and family, the figures were cut out and mounted on white paper, constructing snippets of nightmares, a narrative of all the ways disabled girls and women were abused by the world: a creepy man with overly long arms reaching into the bed of a girl sleeping, her wheelchair beside the bed; a family clustered around a hospital bed, the IVs and tubes removed from the woman lying down, her friend, another woman in a wheelchair, watching and crying; a wheelchair hung by a noose from a tree, a girl with braids and arms akimbo falling through the air to the ground. I drew all of these silhouettes freehand, except for one—I couldn't get the shape of the woman watching her friend dying to look right, and so I placed myself between the projector and the paper, and had Katie trace me.

I was beginning to understand the dark outlines of some stories.

As a nod to the first piece of Walker's that I saw, I titled my piece *Caught! Or, an unfortunate narrative told from a heart between two wheels.* It was hung at a local community-center-turned-gallery for a short time, and I invited my art class crush to the opening because I believed baring all this pain was a way to make him want me. I don't remember if he showed, but I am inclined to think he didn't because I do remember retreating to a separate room to cry and am pretty sure it was in response to a "Sorry I won't actually be able to make it after all" text. Of course this was partly just teenage angst. But given the mural in the other room and my closeness to the darkness portrayed in it, it seems unfair and untrue to assign the cause of my tears simply to *average teenage emotion*, whatever that phrase actually means.

December 19XX

My parents began to suspect something was different about my development as a baby because I never tried to pull myself up into a standing position. I don't know if I tried to and couldn't, or if I somehow intrinsically knew my legs wouldn't be able to support me. Typical developmental milestones delayed or missed—*typical* a word agreed to mean specific characteristics and abilities.

Eventually, my grandma sent information to my mom about Spinal Muscular Atrophy, telling her she thinks she should look at it. My mom doesn't. She lets the pages of information sit in their fax machine, untouched and unread. She didn't want to see the future because of what she thought it would mean. Milestones delayed or missed, timelines less lines and more backtracks and swoops.

In my mind, most insistent throughout my growing up was not a timeline of physical development but one of romantic relationships and dating. Most of my non-disabled peers started dating, and I didn't. My non-disabled friends had their first kisses, and I didn't. My timeline made no sense to me. Clearly, something was wrong.

Of course this was only part of the story. I know more people, now, both with visible disabilities and those without, who experienced different facets of romance and sexuality and various moments in their lives, not at all in line with the "normal" timeline I perceived everyone following when I was growing up. Some have been much younger than I was when I first started dating and exploring my sexuality, and some have been older. Some don't date, and some don't have sex, both of these valid ways of being. The timeline I'd envisioned has less of a hold in reality than I, at least, was led to believe.

NOVEMBER 20XX

There is, of course, the example of time crawling to a halt and then accelerating to warp speed while the needle pokes my side. Even before I started allowing myself to be given a sedative and painkiller before receiving Spinraza injections, chemicals which fogged my mind and made time bubble, seconds expanded into heavy days within the four walls of the procedure room.

A nurse will play "Nobody Knows" by the Lumineers for me during one injection, and the line expressing how nobody knows the ending to this story will follow me into the future, over and over again.

February 20xx

Other moments that time warped:

My mind skittering out in a classroom in Iowa City when visiting writer Kiese Laymon asked where we wanted to be in ten years, because this was a future distance I had only thought of in hypotheticals bordering on fantasies. *I don't know,* I thought, as I felt my eyes fill. *I don't know what that looks like because I have never visualized myself growing up, I mean* really *growing up.* So much of my life revolves around being able to plan the next step simply because my day-to-day living depends on other people. Still, I have a difficult time trying to plan too far in advance—is this a "too late to die young" legacy, or looking at the apparent face of humanity teetering on the brink?

In my bedroom, March 2020, the world colliding as I cry to my two friends who are with me, "People aren't taking it seriously," and they assure me people are, but then look what happened. Anything and everything disabled people predicted.

On the beaten dirt under a shelter in the middle of Kansas, as the Kaw Nation (also known as the Kanza), a federally recognized Native American tribe with land in Oklahoma and Kansas, held their summer ceremonial dance. I sat next to my friend, herself a Kaw Nation citizen, who I had seen in person for the first time not thirty minutes before as we spotted each other and waved across the makeshift parking lot of flattened grass. We had met through a Zoom writing workshop series that I had hosted the previous summer for disabled writers and had kept in touch and FaceTimed frequently since. Now, sitting next to her, I watched the bright colors from the dancers' attire swirl and sway to the chanting coming from the circle of dark-skinned men around a drum in the center.

The sun set far too quickly. Sarah and I had driven an hour and a half from Lawrence to attend the dance, and because my helpers would be switching off around 11 p.m., and because my bedtime routine takes as long as it does, it was suddenly time to leave after it felt like we had just gotten there.

"Time moves differently at dances," my friend said to me when I told her that Sarah and I had to start driving back. In the Kaá^{n}ze Íe (Kanza) language, there are only two tenses, and time is expressed differently than it is in English. There is the now and the not now, the actual and the potential. The potential future (the not now) allows life to happen. The actual (the now) encompasses the past, everything that has already happened up to this point (although this explanation still relies on a separation of past and present, a separation not a part of Kaáⁿze Íe language). "Those things that happened to our ancestors and to our land are still present tense, although we may add the word 'then' in a sentence to explain that it happened before the now," my friend told me. "The language doesn't allow things to die, because in our culture, being and not being are one and the same." It is no surprise, then, that the experience of the dance bent to a different clock.

Two of these moments are akin to the shrinking I feel in the middle of a panic attack, the other is something entirely different. What I'm saying is, you can be out of time and out of time, both meanings. What I'm saying is, I'm not sure you can be both simultaneously. What I'm saying is, one moment stretched into another and another. And they still have not arrived at an ending.

September 20XX

After *Caught!* had been displayed, my parents carefully put it in our basement, where the shapes of terror lay between cement and blankets for however many odd years, before I decided there was no good way to preserve it, and we took it to the recycling.

Caught! portrayed a moment preserved forever in time, like a photograph—the photo of me as a baby reaching for the camera, or the photo of me as a kid with my arms wrapped protectively around a toddler Sarah, or the photo of my back just after surgery, the scar yellowed and bandages peeling with dried blood.

In the artist's statement which hung next to *Caught! Or, an unfortunate narrative told from a heart between two wheels* I wrote,

> I don't pretend to have included all the horrors females with disabilities have gone through in this piece, and I certainly don't pretend to

> know everything about the ones I have expressed. I only know what I myself have experienced. I call this piece *Caught!* because it is, in a sense, a frozen piece of time, an instant where so many crimes and evils are about to be committed. You, the viewer, have arrived, and not a moment too soon.

It's not a new idea, but art—including Kara Walker's—doesn't just capture a moment but also ensures its immortality. It stops time and stretches it. The nightmare caricatures of Walker's work force viewers to reckon with how the effects of slavery and racism live on, how this very American atrocity does not simply live in the past, is not relegated to a specific range of years.

When I made *Caught!*, the silhouettes were a manifestation of the new ways I was coming to terms with reality at that point in my life. Which is to say, I made the ugliness of previous experiences into a story that I could understand and share with others. Which is to say, I had no understanding, at this time, of how mirroring *Caught!* with *Gone* bordered on equating racism with ableism, and how this erases the experiences of disabled people of color, or in this specific instance, the very particular horrors experienced by Black disabled women. A quote from writer Keah Brown: "Non-Black disabled people who equate every ableist thing to racism: do you ever tire? Your long threads and hot takes always seem to forget that Black disabled people exist. We do. We aren't just going to tuck ourselves away to fit your narrative."

Gone was Walker's first work that catapulted her into fame and the art circles of New York City. Perhaps not surprisingly, it came with a large amount of controversy. In 1997, the same year she became the youngest person to ever receive a MacArthur Foundation Fellowship, Walker was criticized for using racial stereotypes in her artwork by a group of older, Black artists. Others have defended her style, and pointed to the very narrow roles Black artists are seemingly allowed to occupy.

Caught! preserved a story in time, freezing a moment while stretching it into the future. And although we discarded the paper shapes and silhouettes, the story is being invoked here, again in black and white, this time ink on paper. This is an attempt to occupy a new space.

January 20XX

Alison Kafer also writes of "No Future for Crips," building upon queer theorists' explorations of how the future is often withheld from those outside of heteronormative identities and relationships, whether this be through oppression and lack of life-giving resources, or through the intricate arguments surrounding queer folks and children—either they're bad parents or fully capable. Either way, it's nearly impossible to "conceive of a future without the figure of the Child," an idea argued by queer theorist Lee Edelman, whose work builds on the work of another famed theorist, Lauren Berlant.

What if you're also disabled? What if, like being gay and having kids, there are arguments swirling around disability and parenting? What if these arguments often paint disabled parents as truly selfish people? What if you don't want to bear children but also don't want your people to disappear, both in the present and in years to come?

August 20XX

My coping mechanisms are both unique and altogether common. The pages in my notebook are taken up by more and more prayers, less poems and lists—pleas for safety and health and patience. All supplications start with the same sentence, anyway: *please keep us safe, please keep us healthy, please keep us sane.* I am back home in Iowa, in our backyard meadow as plants reach for the sunlight of late morning.

I keep trying to identify more species on the plant identification apps I keep downloading, but there is something that feels so very human about it, by which I mean just because I am learning the name of a plant and saving that to my phone does not mean I have tamed it, despite what *The Little Prince* would tell us. The baby oaks still dance in the breeze, whether I've noticed they are there or not.

My anxiety, also, continues to morph and change shape. When I was back in Kansas in the spring and a helper was sick, I was so terrified they had COVID I went into a shutdown spiral in my bedroom. There was more to it than this—my helper didn't want to get tested, and that also kicked my hurt and panic into high gear. I had called a good friend in a complete state of numbness and dissociation, but they didn't pick up.

Now, here, in the meadow, late August. Nearly a year and a half into the pandemic, nearly twenty-seven years into my life. How do we measure time, really? Vaccinated people test positive more frequently now, it seems, and I don't react except to allow myself to feel solace in our backyard which is less of a yard and certainly not a lawn—it is everything a lawn is not.

In the heat from the sun, I can feel my blood slow in its flow through my body, as if I am attempting to become one with the lives around me in other forms. The plants growing beside me move at a speed closer to Crip time, a term used to acknowledge the way disabled bodyminds may move through the world at different rates. Despite the sadness of the pandemic weighing heavy, this is, truly, what I know best about contentment. This is the best way to spend a morning, letting words dissolve into the meadow and on the tip of my tongue, like sugar breaking down in the wetness of my mouth.

May 19xx

SMA is definitive—its proof, so to speak, lies in the way my genes are built, which is of course to say in the ways my genes are not built. Its proof is in the construction and deconstruction of a way the body internally communicates. And yet, I was not diagnosed until I was sixteen months old, which means that prior to this diagnosis, I *was* and was *not*. The naming of the way my body inhabited the world made no internal difference to my body and bodymind—although it did impact how others saw me and did not see me, how they interacted and did not interact with me, and in some way, then, this acted as a mirror through which to see myself.

I wonder about myself before sixteen months—both younger and in utero. Did I exist out of time? As in, not within the realm of what we, as humans, have decided time is? And when I got to twenty-four months, was Death suddenly told, "Sorry, you've ran out of time to collect her. Try again later"?

March 20xx

And then midnight struck, and the clock stopped ticking.

I Don't Know the Difference Between Beginnings and Endings

In Iowa, halfway through April and two months into the pandemic, it snows overnight. My parents come to wake me up at 9 a.m. so that I will be ready to hold a Zoom call with my students at 11, and as my mom opens the blinds of my window she says, "Guess what? It's white outside." By the time I am sitting at the makeshift desk in front of my bedroom window, opening up Zoom, most of the snow has melted, although there is still a thin layer on the branches of trees and roofs of houses in our neighborhood. Directly outside my window is our front porch, and directly in front of this are three barberry bushes, whose red buds are just starting to push forth. But this morning, the red is covered in white, and if you squint your eyes the bushes are in full bloom, bright with snow-white petals.

The day before, my mom asked me about my levels of anxiety. "I feel fine," I said, truthfully. "There's usually one day, about every other week, where I feel down, but that's more depression, I would say." Also true, although now, as we near the middle of May, my days of sadness are much more frequent. The week before April's first snow, I had sat in front of my computer, watching Harry Styles's Tiny Desk Concert through NPR, and cried. The world, I was certain, was going to end because of the vast disappointment that is the human race, and my childhood bedroom was going to be the place in which I drew my final breath as we all went up in (figurative or literal) flames.

But still, this is a deep sadness that I feel, a grieving for what I am loath to say goodbye to, not fear. I came home from Kansas for spring break and suddenly realized I would be home for much longer than I had initially planned. The sadness invoked by this knowledge curls around the sadness of knowing I will someday have to say goodbye—if not to this life, then to Iowa, even if temporarily.

My lack of fear in the beginning of the pandemic is odd, I suppose, given how fearful the majority of those around me have become. My grandparents live down the street from the house I grew up in, the house I shelter in with my parents before getting vaccinated. This is an especially difficult time for them. Over a family Zoom call one night, my grandpa tells us all (cousins and aunts and uncles spread from Portland to Des Moines to Kansas City to Chicago to Minneapolis) that in the past six weeks he has left the house twice, each time for a doctor's appointment.

His comment about not leaving the house for six weeks reads as funny, because my grandpa bursts into laughter after telling us, but it's also indicative of a larger fear: the world as he has known it has finally turned upside down, topsy-turvy, it's all going to hell in a handbasket and if the COVID-19 virus were to lodge inside his body, or inside his wife's body, it would all likely be over. At least, this is how we interpret his actions, the story we have chosen to tell.

At this point, I believe that if I were to contract the virus, I also would likely not survive. I have been receiving spinal injections of Spinraza for the past year and a half, and I think (I hope) that my lungs have gotten incrementally stronger. But strong enough to overcome COVID-19-induced pneumonia? Maybe, but probably not.

And yet, this possibility doesn't scare me. Of course, I am saying this now, in full health, the potential of being robbed of breath distant from my current reality. For such a long period of my life, getting sick with respiratory-related illnesses was one of my biggest triggers of anxiety. I don't know how our fears and emotions change, but it seems that somewhere over the course of the past year, this dark, heavy weight has fallen away from me. Harriet McBryde Johnson wrote in *Too Late to Die Young,* "I've accepted the reality of death so early it's hard to imagine life without it." This makes sense to me.

During a Zoom conference for one of my graduate classes, I tell my professor that I feel very detached from it all, when she asks how I am feeling about the current COVID-19 situation. "And why do you think that is?" she asks. "Because you have been preparing for this your whole life?" At first I'm taken aback by this, before realizing it holds a certain truth. The "this" my professor is referring to is death—failing of the body, *failing* perhaps being the wrong word because this *is* what we're ultimately meant to do, right? This *is* how our bodies are meant to end. It might happen with this pandemic, and it very well might not.

I wonder, sometimes, to what extent we have turned my grandfather into a character in a story—the man who lived through the Great Depression, who served in the army (although not in combat), who was a Park Ranger for the National Park Service. The year before my grandparents got married, my grandpa was working at Olympic National Park in Port Angeles, Washington. Olympic is my mom's favorite National Park ("It has everything," she tells me).

I didn't have to ask for the following story, don't remember when I first heard it, which I suppose is indicative of how much his stories fed my childhood, along with the childhoods of his six other grandchildren.

There was a man that was staying at a campground in the park, who liked to follow my grandpa around and say disconcerting things. One day, my grandpa was on a rickety bridge over a ravine and somehow found himself accompanied by this man. "This would be a good place to kill someone," the man had said, to which my grandpa thought, *Okay, I better get away from here lickity-split.*

This story has always been accompanied by great bouts of laughter—it's one I still tell my friends on road trips to new places and new sights, pre-pandemic. But now, it makes me think of a line from *Among the Living and the Dead*, a book by Inara Verzemnieks, the writing professor in undergrad who recommended *The Argonauts* to me. In *Among the Living and the Dead,* Inara travels to Latvia to trace her family's history, staying with her great-aunt and great-uncle. She spent a lot of time interviewing her great-aunt, her grandma's sister, who had been separated from her grandma during World War II. Oftentimes, Inara's great-uncle would come in from outside during an interview, and in an attempt to distract his wife from the sadness she was telling, would cut in with, "Have I told you how many times I should have died?" *Have I told you how many times I should have died?*

A story I don't hear until I ask my grandparents for it: When my mom and her older brother were toddlers (there were still two more kids to come), my grandpa was assigned to work at Lookout Point in Sequoia National Park in California. When you're assigned a job and place, my grandma would explain to me now, the house comes with it. And this house was up at the very top of a mountain, where two roads converged, with not much room around it for, say, two small children to safely play. My grandma looked around at the trees and the dirt and the house and the edge of the mountain, not necessarily a drop-off, but not a gentle slope either, and thought, *This isn't going to work.*

That night, my grandparents, mom, and uncle slept on sleeping bags rolled out on the floor of the house. This would be the only night they would spend in that house. The following morning, they would wake up, roll up their sleeping bags, and all drive back down the mountain. I suppose it could have been either my grandma or my grandpa who told the ranger station their family needed to be reassigned, but it was undoubtedly thanks to my grandma that the reassignment happened.

When they tell me this story over FaceTime, we all laugh at the absurdity and wonderfulness that was their life. "I was a bad father!" my grandpa says, and although he is laughing, I don't think he is joking.

"No, no, don't say that," my grandma cuts in. "Those experiences and times shaped who we were."

My grandpa was reassigned to a different part of the park, a different temporary home, to work as a fire marshal, and my mom and uncle were left to play in the grass and the mud surrounding the cluster of park ranger houses that they had been moved to.

My grandma grew up in Mason City, Illinois. The town had a population of just under 2,000 in 1940, the same year she was born. Her best friend, Jolly, was the daughter of the director of the funeral home that my grandma, Sue, lived across the street from. "I suppose it was always present in my awareness, because of this," my grandma tells me over a FaceTime call one morning—it, of course, being death.

Two sisters drowned in the pond right outside of town, when my grandma was in first or second grade. I spend hours trying to find the obituaries of the girls in Mason City newspapers, and when I come up with nothing, I send a text to my grandma, confirming the spelling of their last name: Cleery? *I think their name was Cleary,* she responds. *It was a long time ago.*

But even with that spelling, I can't find them.

By April 20, Iowa becomes one of the eight states to not issue a statewide stay-at-home order. The eighth week of being home with my parents finds my mom and me on our back deck, painting "SAVE LIVES, stay home" on a PETE FOR AMERICA sign that we have turned inside out, so that the blue and yellow of his campaign are hidden beneath solid black. I had volunteered for Elizabeth Warren's campaign over winter break and was heartbroken when she finally dropped out of the race. I had convinced my parents to caucus for Warren (an activity I was unable to do, being in Kansas), but really, we all didn't know who the best candidate would be, who was most likely to defeat 45. We ended up with multiple signs in our yard.

Now, we daubed beige house paint to form letters that would be bold enough to read from the street, and outlined the words in purple, teal, and orange. The entire time we are doing this, I can sense that my mom is unhappy, on edge, worn out. There's a moment when she snaps and I feel tears tug at the back of my throat, emotion that has been waiting all day for a chance to spill beyond the boundaries of my body.

She has just returned from my grandparents' house, less than a mile up the road from ours. Because we have a cat at my parents' house who is overwhelmingly timid, I keep Mercury at my grandparents whenever I come home. The first few weeks of isolation, I still went over to my grandparents nearly every day, in part to talk with them, in part to coax Mercury to lay down on my chest. Recently, though, I've stopped visiting them because it doesn't seem strictly necessary, and therefore not worth the risk. It's why, for example, I've decided to interview them for an essay I'm working on with two screens between us. It's the early days of the pandemic, when it still seems likely the virus spreads on surfaces, and we define activities as those which are absolutely necessary and those which aren't.

My mom, however, continues to walk to their house daily, masked and gloved and six feet away from them when possible, because, like me, they need help. Unlike me, the reliance on others is not yet something they are accustomed to. My uncle also lives with them, a blessing in times like these when the amount my mom can do is limited. Still, it is an adjustment for them, an adjustment that would have marched into their life with or without the pandemic, an adjustment they are sometimes resistant to, a feeling I both relate to personally and don't. I accepted the reality of death when I was a kid, just as I accepted (sometimes begrudgingly) the fact that I needed help from others.

We finish painting the sign. I tell my mom I have to use the bathroom, and we gather up art supplies to carry inside.

"I'm sorry," my mom says as soon as she comes into the bathroom to help me. "I'm sorry I was acting like that." I assure her she is fine, that we all have days like this, especially now. I know from the way the light hits her eyes that there are pools of tears waiting. I know this because I grew up learning how to be attuned to what others are feeling, particularly if we were living in the same house—in the years after my dad stopped drinking and was still evolving into sobriety, I would sometimes feel myself transforming into a buffer between my parents' emotions, a transformation I have had to learn, now, to let go of.

"It's just that I can't help my mom and dad more," she says, and then the water rises and falls, scooting in droplets down her nose.

"I know," I say. She lifts me onto the table and then onto my bathroom chair. "I know, I know, and it's okay."

But the facts piling up to create this exact moment are not okay, and here's why: The state of Tennessee has policies in place from 2016 regarding (among other things) hospital admission during a pandemic. Under the section "Triage Tools and Tables," see: "(a) Exclusion Cri-

TERIA for Hospital Admission: The patient is excluded from admission or transfer to critical care if ANY of the following is present:

"Option 7: Advanced untreatable neuromuscular disease (such as ALS, end-stage MS, spinal muscular atrophy) requiring assistance with activities of daily living or requiring chronic ventilatory support."

I find this while doing research for an article I am writing on marginalized bodies and COVID-19. I highlight "spinal muscular atrophy" and screenshot the page. A few weeks later, I sort through the images and files crowding the desktop of my laptop and drag what no longer interests me to the trashcan at the bottom of the screen. For some reason, I let this picture stay.

It's harder to pinpoint where my grandparents would fall on Tennessee's scale of worth, but, as noted physician and public health researcher Atul Gawande has noted, aging is an "accumulation" of various cellular mutations, damages, and problems. What Gawande doesn't say, but what I, along with countless disability scholars, will: aging is an accumulation of disabilities, an accumulation, perhaps, that translates to this chart.

In February 2021, the BBC will report that nearly 60 percent of COVID deaths in the UK are of people with disabilities, a fact I stumble across on Twitter. While looking through the retweets of the article, I see a Tweet of someone saying that this statistic is misrepresenting the facts, because the majority of that percentage were elderly individuals, not young or middle-aged people with disabilities. But this is what a culture that profits off of able-bodiedness doesn't want you to know: the elderly and the disabled are not two distinct groups; they exist on a continuum. You age and acquire disabilities, or you are already disabled and outlive the age our culture has assumed. The data from the article, also, tells a different story than this person's Tweet: Even when age is taken into account through something called "age-standardized mortality rates," the rate of COVID-19 related deaths in disabled individuals was statistically significantly higher.

The exclusion criteria are the policies put in place in Tennessee, not Iowa, but the acceptance of this value system is the same across the country, not just apparent in our governmental systems, but also from person to person. There is, for example, the photo of a lockdown protester that circulates social media: they are holding a sign that says, "SACRIFICE THE WEAK."

A month after my mom and I finish painting our yard signs, almost to the day, disability activist Stacey Park Milbern dies on her thirty-third birthday due to complications from a surgery to remove kidney cancer that had been postponed because of stay-at-home orders. Milbern helped found the Disability Justice movement, which calls for a radical intersectional approach to disability activism and works to create spaces of true care and access outside of the systems that have caused so many people so much harm. Milbern was a queer, disabled, Korean American woman. When the pandemic hit, Milbern and a group of other activists in the Bay Area put together kits that included hand sanitizers, respirators, and disinfectants and distributed them to unhoused people. She posted a video shortly before she died discussing the inequitable care disabled people—especially disabled people of color—would likely receive (or not receive) because of the pandemic. Stacey Park Milbern wasn't an oracle; she was a brilliant individual who lived her life authentically and was loved by many. She was human, and that's enough for her to deserve to be heard.

During another FaceTime call with my grandparents, I'm sitting outside on our back porch (today, temperatures have reached mid-seventies) when the generator we have connected to our house starts with a noise like a lawnmower being revved. The *grgrgrgrgrgr* startles me, and I tell my grandparents I am going to move inside so we can hear each other easier. My grandpa is already very hard of hearing, and my voice, always raised when talking to him, reaches the level of shouting: "We won't be able to hear each other, let me go inside and call you back!"

The generator runs for fifteen minutes once a week, as part of some sort of maintenance routine it must go through to be prepared for when it's actually needed. We have the generator because of the medical equipment I need—like the generator, my two breathing machines are used normally for maintenance purposes only, to keep my lungs pliable and my blood well-fed with oxygen. But if I get sick, these routines become, quite literally, a matter of life and death.

When I move my computer inside to the same makeshift desk in front of my bedroom window where I Zoom with my students, I try calling my grandma's iPad again through FaceTime—the only way we can talk like this, her phone pre-smart phone, their old desktop computer just that: old. My grandpa, like my dad, does not have a cell phone.

I can't get the call to connect, and for a few tries I am simply given the "Grandma's iPad is unavailable for FaceTime" message. When I finally get through, though, Mercury has jumped onto my grandpa's chest and is giving him his signature cat hug, something that entails him placing each paw on either side of your neck, sometimes both paws on the same shoulder. From here, he climbs up onto my grandpa's shoulders and back and looks down at the iPad.

"I am not as fearful for myself as I am for other people," my grandma says when I ask her about what it would mean for her to contract Covid-19. "I am more fearful for the young people." I wonder, then, if she means me. Although my grandparents know nothing of O., the girl I am virtually dating at this time and crushing hard on, a girl with a severely weakened immune system, it strikes me that my grandma could also be talking about her. There are, of course, so many ways to interpret what she's said.

My grandpa, it turns out, is not as fearful as we thought, or if he is, he's not letting on: "Most days I don't think about it," and "I'm healthy enough, I think, to recover from it." I don't know if he is in denial, or if he's simply made peace with his own mortality and therefore is willing to just be content with the present.

My grandma is supposed to have her hip replaced in April, but our governor decides this is a nonessential surgery (bowling alleys, take note, remain open) and so she isn't able to have it done until June. She's in so much pain we arrange to get her a tincture of THC, which she says helps. When she does finally have surgery, the surgeon tells her that her hip has been broken, likely for the past few months. My grandma is one of the strongest women I know, but I want strength to be more than just enduring pain.

My grandma will fall in September and have to get her other hip replaced, and then again in November, this time breaking her femur. She has surgery the day that Biden is finally declared the forty-sixth president, and when I text her in the hospital to say that I'm sending her lots of love and healing, and that even though something terrible happened, we still got to witness Biden being announced winner, she responds with *I was just thinking that that was going to be the really big, bright memory for the day! And 4 years from now maybe we will have a woman president. Love you.*

Later that day, my mom will tell me that my grandma had confided to her months earlier that she did not think she would live to see Trump out of office. In the flowers I order her from my cousins and me, I have the card include the message: *Get well vibes on this historic day!* and include Biden's name in the list of people the flowers are from. Internally, I still wish we had someone more progressive as our candidate, but by the time inauguration rolls around, Biden has already announced his comprehensive plan to address the pandemic, and considering 94 percent of COVID-19 deaths have been of people with pre-existing conditions *and* the disproportionate effect the pandemic has had on people of color and people of lower socioeconomic classes, this is no small thing. Shortly after he takes office, it is reported that the pandemic response plan left by Trump wasn't *bad*—it was nonexistent.

It is decided that my grandma will need a wheelchair when she returns from the hospital, and so the battle with her insurance company begins. It is decided, also, that keeping Mercury with my grandparents is too risky, that his rambunctiousness, which had thankfully not been the cause of any falls, was too likely to cause future problems, and that he'll need to come live with us, separated from our other cat. Eventually, after four months of our other cat living primarily in the basement and acting terrified of Mercury, they begin to hang out together in a way that resembles tolerance, a scene we never could have predicted.

To keep my grandparents' spirits up, we take Mercury over to their house for visits, during which he'll romp around their house, curl up on the couch and fall asleep, or climb onto their laps and give them his signature hugs.

We buy my grandma a puzzle highlighting key figures in the women's suffrage movement for her birthday and then work on it with her, the colorful pieces scattered over their dining room table. "Every time I wheel past the table, I tell them thank you," she tells us each time we go over.

I'm sitting eating dinner with my parents one night at the beginning of the pandemic when my mom makes a comment about the newness of certain feelings, a newness that seems to be facilitated by the pandemic. She has read about this newness in an article shared with her by my brother. "It's like when I went to the store last, and there were so many things gone off the shelves, so many empty spaces. I noticed I had this physical reaction to seeing this, like a panicky feeling. It's new."

I have felt a total of zero new emotions because of this, I thought, even as I was thinking that what my mom surely meant was that the *cause* of the panic was new, not the panic itself. This won't be true for much longer, as with each passing week I will begin to more fully understand how explicit and deeply entrenched disregard for disabled life is.

The week after spring break, the week that's been set aside for us all to make the transition to online classes, I get in touch with four of my writer friends and ask them—without trying to sound too morbid—if they will be in charge of getting my work out in the world if I die. Throughout all of this, I am unusually calm, unusually indifferent. I make a folder in my Google Drive and put all my writing from the past three years in it, knowing that if I need to, I can hit "share," enter their four email addresses, and rest easy. Posthumous books sell better anyway—everyone loves writing from beyond the grave.

It's the end of week seven, now, and what I have yet to do in my preparation for the end is to write up my preferences for *before* death. It occurs to me suddenly that this is something I have very much not made peace with: the unavoidable decline that precedes the final goodbye. My mom has ordered these pamphlets called "Five Wishes," something she read about it Atul Gawande's *Being Mortal,* and when I read through one while eating lunch one day, I am presented with options such as "I want to be taken off all life-giving equipment and medicine if it appears I will not recover," or "I want to be taken off all life-giving equipment and medicine if doctors say there is nothing as that can be reasonably done to improve my condition."

I don't spend too much time deciding which of these I prefer, because the language leaves things too open to chance, too dependent on interpretation: When I read these two options, I'm reminded of the man in the Facebook group I'm in for adults with neuromuscular diseases, who, years back had gone to the hospital for a run-of-the-mill sickness and had noticed that his wristband had DNR on it, a Do Not Resuscitate order ordered without his knowledge or consent.

In the future, I will be preparing to return to Kansas after being vaccinated and will metaphorically put my face in my hands at the stress of trying to arrange a schedule for my helpers that works for everyone involved. When I text my helper and friend Sierra to tell her that figuring out the logistics is always tough, she responds, *It is tough, but just think—you're coming home!* I'm not, though. Perhaps one of my homes, a temporary home I have learned to love, but not *home.*

And then, also, this: since I first moved away from the house in which I grew up, the words *I want to go home* have beaten themselves into my mind in a sort of daily mantra. As mantras go, I realize this is not a positive one, although it is surely true. When I move to Kansas to start grad school, I decide it's time to work on weeding this one out and planting something new—things are already hard enough in this new town and new school, without a daily mental reminder that I don't want to be there. But this is harder, perhaps, than it appears. After the pandemic has broken out and classes have moved online for the rest of the semester and I am home

(home!) in Iowa, I still can't get this mantra out of my head, and I begin to wonder where its longing is directed.

In a memory I have carefully wrapped up, placed in a box, and put high on a shelf, I cried "I want to go home!" over and over in my bedroom, in between cycles of air being pushed into my lungs from the cough assist machine, something I didn't have the muscle strength to do unaided. I had a respiratory something or other, an itch at the back of my throat that had turned to pain and then fluid in my airways. I was in fourth grade and it was the Saturday morning of our spring break. My body had become something I wanted to crawl away from. In that moment, I knew what home meant—I no longer wanted to be alive.

The fact that my parents experienced their daughter being so sick she told them she wanted to die pains me to an extent that I no longer wish to die before they do, as excruciating as that may be for me. In the weeks that I'm stuck in Iowa, I decide to rebuild my understanding of "the ruin that has become our collective home," as anthropologist Anna Tsing says of our postwar, industrialized, capitalist society. I want to be able to exist in a place without longing to leave it.

On May 2, at the end of the eighth week of me being home in Iowa, my grandmother's best friend, Jolly, dies after a dance with cancer. It's a reminder, I suppose, that death is continuing to make the normal rounds, pandemic or not. "But we know, despite the feelings a writer possesses upon writing a beginning, that endings happen, that beginnings do indeed come to an end," writer Jenny Boully says. "The book spine betrays; the wordcount a demise; each page number a crossing out of calendar days."

Both of my grandparents tell me at different times during our interviews that the fear lies in the uncertainty—the uncertainty of the Great Depression, the wars they lived through, and now this virus. Of course we don't understand death—no more so, I think, than we understand love, or home, or how our lives are irrevocably shaped by who and what we encounter.

It snows two more times in April. One morning, my helper pulls open the blinds in my bathroom and says, "What the?" There are reportedly three inches of snow on the ground in central Iowa, and although it doesn't stick around into the afternoon, it's another one of those not-so-subtle reminders that the rules which perhaps have governed our existence are slowly losing their grip on this reality.

The pond in which the two sisters drowned during my grandma's childhood is the same pond on which she learns to ice skate the year she and my grandpa start dating. She doesn't know, on that night in the middle of winter, with a fire built by both of them to light up the dark on the island in the middle of the pond, if she thought of the two sisters who had died in the same spot where she was now, possibly, falling in love.

She does think, though, that each time she'd driven past that pond in the twenty-three years that she lived in Mason City, she likely remembered those two sisters.

Once, in the same grass where my mom and uncle played at Sequoia National Park, there was a rattlesnake that another ranger living in this same area found and killed. There were many snakes in this area, but only this one was deadly. Before he killed it, though, he wanted my grandma to look at it.

"I don't want to see it!" she told him, to which he did not listen.

"You need to look at it," he told her, "so you know what to look for in the future."

DREAM

The Bystander

You have a dream one night that you are in a dark room, dark like the brain matter oozing from the doctor's skull in another room in another dream. There is a vat of chemicals that is keeping a ~~human~~ ~~animal~~ creature alive or maybe it's actually killing it or maybe the whole thing is taking place to see if cells can be commanded to grow and multiply and change and submit and lay down and roll over and take it and get on their knees. You know you're not the one operating the mechanism keeping chemicals pumping into the vat but you are crumpled over, guilt turning your insides inside out, in spite of this.

MERMAID INTERLUDE

The Fourth Mermaid

We transitioned to living online because of the plague, something that seemed outside of the king's control. What I mean is, he couldn't hold the sickness in his hands and didn't understand, then, how he could end it. What I mean is, we soon found out the kingdom's top health officials had told the king about the advent of the plague and policies he could enforce to contain it, and he outright refused. Yes, the kingdom had health officials. I don't pretend to know how the government worked, just that in this kingdom death can be performed, but is also very real.

The plague spread as much by a diffusion of misinformation and conspiracy as it did by infected fleas. The king made a smear campaign of the health officials, after it was revealed that they had advised him to act differently. Eventually, the mermaids would become another scapegoat, one which would, of course, make no logical sense. But there was a stark contrast between the public's response to the besmirching of health officials and then the villainizing of us, beings who were apparently not human enough to be saved. Doctors, health officials, *the medical complex*—just as the veracity of such institutions were being questioned, another campaign took off to bolster them and keep the kingdom safe. All in the name of science.

And while I certainly understood the need for the counter campaign (a counter *narrative*), the image that kept returning to my mind's eye was the one doctor I had gone to when I first felt scales poking through the skin on my legs: looking down at me over his glasses, "Scales? No, no, that can't be, I'm sorry to say this, my dear, but you must be imagining it. By which I mean it is not your fault, your mind is just playing tricks on you." And the next doctor, this one a woman: "Oh yes, I have read of this occurrence. Highly fascinating from a scientific standpoint. My best guess would be that on a cellular level you are no longer compatible with many of the sensory inputs essential to humankind, so, in a way, your cells are rebelling." And the next one, of which their gender really made no difference: "Tails! Mermaid tails! Punishment, perhaps? Or an outlying symptom of the plague? Do you, to the best of your knowledge, remember any itchy bumps around your ankles from the past few weeks? Flea bites, you understand." I understood. I had only felt safe going to the doctors because I was one of the first to transform. Once there were more of us, the outrage took over, and we spent our time in hiding.

The one profession not included in the counter campaign to bolster the credibility of science and medicine was that of the village witch. It wouldn't have looked good from a PR standpoint, I suppose, to group her in with the rest of them. She was a threat to the system, get it? But I'd hear from another mermaid—through the complicated underground system we had configured for communication—that the village witch was the only person who had actually been able to help with the pain of the scale growth, and so one night, before my legs had completely disappeared and I could wear my coat which went down to my knees to hide any of the swelling from the tail, I ventured out to her house.

The mermaid who had directed me to her was in love with this woman, I could tell from how she talked about her. This made me wonder if the witch was being perceived through rose-colored glasses, doubtful as I was at any promise of help. But at this point, I was out of options. When the witch answered my knock, I understood immediately why the other mermaid loved her. She was beautiful and calm and exuded this light that dripped with both sexuality and softness. She gave me a salve and a blanket that sparkled with gold. After the official proclamation against mermaids was issued, I grew fearful for our witch, and knew we would have to do what we could to protect her. If word came around that she was helping us, well, I didn't like to think what would happen.

When the number of plague deaths reached 400,000—when so many deaths had abounded—the schools finally took action and moved everything to online for the remainder of the semester.

The transition to online classes couldn't have come at a better time for me. The camera never captured my lower half, and so I could sit through class after class without anyone knowing I was different from the person they'd last seen on campus, across the table from them in a writing workshop.

I was in an experimental fiction class and our professor kept asking us, does the content necessitate the experiment? Does the content necessitate the form? My mother was an artist, a designer, and she was always going on about *form follows function,* meaning that if the thing or the place *did not work* it didn't matter how beautiful it looked. You understand what I'm getting at, right? If the legs shriveled up, it didn't matter how beautiful the glitter off the scales were which grew in their place.

First, I started writing stories about people who had fish tails instead of legs. Then, I started dreaming about them—prismed mirrors in the hallway reflecting halved bodies, women caught on fish hooks glistening with blood and the sea, and always, as if my subconscious was being haunted by a gatekeeping demon, a voice echoing through the background of these scenes: *get out, get out, get out.* I didn't get out. I stayed. I needed to witness the story.

I'd been cautious of writing things down since the incident with the girl I loved—I should have never cemented that desire into words on a page, should have kept it sheltered within me, unformed in language. I'd realized, after this, that writing something down can make it a reality, can usher in an avalanche of calamity that comes along with truth. I realized this, too, when I spoke my words allowed to this woman—not just the words of my love, but the words about my writing: *The people on the page . . . I created them and thus they are real.* Still, I never believed this would apply to mermaids. It would have been a mark of insanity, wouldn't it, to predict that putting scaly tails onto paper would result in a morning when I could no longer feel my legs because, in fact, they were no longer there.

Skeletons

MONDAY: I am moving on Saturday. I am moving to a new town and new state which means I am leaving this town and this state and this home. I am moving, and I am terrible at goodbyes.

I am packing in fits and spurts. One day, I take out all of the boxes that a neighbor has lent me and space them out evenly over the living room floor. They are empty, for now.

I am moving and I am trying to write a fictionalized story about the terrors of change for the short story collection my friend and I are compiling, but I don't know how to do this and so I simply tell the truth. Sometimes, though, truth looks a lot like fiction, and fiction looks a lot like the truth.

When I sit down at my laptop between bouts of packing, I lay my hand flat on the keyboard and realize it looks dead, like something that doesn't belong to me, but instead a corpse found in the woods, the body of a girl abducted and betrayed and left for someone else to find. I keep reading "Mo Mháistir Dorcha/My Dark Master," a Nuala Ní Dhomhnaill poem which the man I thought I loved cooed over.

> *I've gone and hired myself out. I've hired myself out to death [. . .]*
> *"What a stroke of luck," he declared,*
> *"when a master who's set on a maid finds himself a maid who's set*
> *on a master."*

I am over two weeks late for my period—there is nothing growing inside of me,* though, only knots of stress. Perhaps my body is panicking at the thought of uprooting. Perhaps my body doesn't know what to do.

**I read a story once about a girl who didn't get her period for an entire year after having her body stolen. She finally asked her doctor about it at the end of the year, and when they sent her to the labs to have her blood drawn and tested for anemia, the lab technician couldn't even find a vein. They thought they did, after about 10 minutes of applying heat to her arms and massaging them, but once they stuck the needle in, nothing came out. So she got sent to a specialist, who sent her to another specialist, who did the one thing all of the doctors should have done to begin with and tried to find her pulse. She didn't have one.*

TUESDAY: When I am not packing or trying to write, I spend hours lying on the floor of my kitchen, staring up at the light above me. When I close my eyes, the light doubles against my eyelids and I feel like I'm looking at one of those things you store your contacts in at the end of the day. The man never understood the end of the poem: "What I'll have at the end of the day / I've absolutely no idea, either in terms of three hots and a cot, / or if I'll be allowed to say my say." He would rather I didn't speak.

I don't know what to do about the skeletons in the closet. They're real, not a metaphor, and they don't fit neatly in any of the boxes unless I take them apart. I can't take them apart.

My friends are coming at the end of the week to help me put all the boxes and my couch into the moving truck and the skeletons must be put away securely by then, but I don't know how. When I go stand in front of the closet to look at them, I am overcome by an abundant lack of answers. Sometimes I slide in between them and curl up in the darkness, letting their bones form a weird cloak around me. I am trying, and failing, to tell the truth without slipping into a body that isn't mine.

When I am pressed up against the back wall of the closet, my mind is flooded with memories that make me bite my fist to keep from screaming in pain: the sight of tears running down my dad's cheeks at his friend's funeral, made blurry by my own; the sound my cat made when he was hit by a car, something too human, too close to a dying child; the smell of the room when I walked in on the man I was in love with on top of another woman, a sharp smell, a smell that cut my heart open and made me stumble and gasp *no*.

That man told me I was a masochist. The skeletons in the closet would agree with him.

WEDNESDAY: I am labeling each box* I pack, painstakingly arranging items so that their curves and points and edges fit perfectly together. *VERY FRAGILE KITCHEN* goes in black Sharpie on one—glasses I nicked from restaurants, bowls bought at Goodwill, plates I took from my parents' house. Then there's *BOOKS*, which has Michelle Tea and Maggie Nelson and Carmen Maria Machado, and *KNICKKNACKS*, which has the cat statue and the pens and pencils and picture frames and jewelry and the collar from the cat. There's another kitchen box with half-eaten food. And then there's my suitcase with clothes and another box of *HANGERS + BEDROOM DECORATIONS*. I am putting my travel-sized shampoo, deodorant, toothbrush, and toothpaste in my backpack, along with my laptop and notebook. I have thrown out all of my makeup. Really, I can load all of these boxes into the truck myself. It's the couch I'll need help with. And then, of course, the skeletons are heavier than they look.

**I put pain in boxes, seal the boxes with tape, stack them in the closet.*

THURSDAY: My closet is home to real bone, real human remains. I don't know how the skeletons got here, or maybe I do but don't want to tell. Or maybe my subconscious knows but my conscious does not. Maybe they were put in the closet* when I was gone some day or night or hour.

I wake up in the middle of the night to the sound of their bones knocking against the closet door.

**What if the skeletons end up being more alive than the person whose closet they're living in is? Like, the person who is actually made of flesh and blood and yes, bone, but also so much more than that. What if that person whose closet is home to a collection of skeletons—what if she's not actually powerful enough and by powerful enough I mean human enough and* *by human enough I mean woman enough—what if she can't make the skeletons leave?*

FRIDAY: I can't quite make myself take down the photos and posters from the walls. The feeling of an oncoming apocalypse has settled over me like a net. There is absolutely nothing I can do to stop tomorrow coming. Nothing at all.

Panic is lying low inside me, a thin layer of pulsing fear far under my skin. But by midday, it's merely an annoying distraction, and by evening, a quiet itch.

I put everything I can into boxes. When the only things left are my overnight backpack, mattress, and memories trapped in pictures on the wall, I open the door to the closet. The skulls are leering back at me. For one foolish second, I think of leaving them, digging a hole in the park behind my apartment at night and bidding them good riddance. But of course this is impossible. I read a story once of a girl who buried her skeletons, and before she had shoveled the last scoop of dirt onto their grave, she had turned to stone.

So instead, I lay each skeleton on its back, one on top of the other, in a box I begged the co-op next door for. Their bones touch and make a sorrowful, hollow sound. Before I close the lid over them and tape it shut, I make myself stare into the black shadows where their eyes would be. A vision, then: Skeletons under my bed in my new apartment, skeletons peering around the door, skeletons crawling up to lay beside me and place their dead bone against my flesh. Acid rises, burning, in the back of my throat. I close the lid.

That night, I sleep in a room that is empty save for my mattress and posters on the wall.

SATURDAY: We are loading the boxes into the truck. What is harder to do—leaving a person or leaving a place?

The skeletons are quiet the whole time, even when their box gets jostled by the couch.*

Even if the entire universe rearranged itself so that its star particles were ground particles and humans' cells made up the ocean, even if time stopped moving and showed up in silky star pajamas and said, "I'm quite tired now, I release you, I think I'll be done. May I have a cup of tea?" there are some things you can never stop from happening.

I have the last box in my arms and suddenly the world is threatening to close in around me. The trees are losing their color, the grass seems to be turning brown, the pavement of the parking lot is churning. *Run,* I think. *Run. Run. Run.* My mind latches onto this word and I believe for a split second that this is a logical idea.

But of course there is the new apartment in the new city in the new state and the new job and new people. I hug my friends goodbye. I am climbing into the driver's seat of the truck, the last box beside me. I don't cry because I am still looking out at the world from behind the wall inside of me that's behind my eyes. I feel like I am choking, but the only thing to do is drive.

I turn the key in the ignition and pull away from the curb. *You will like this,* I say to myself about the new apartment in the new city in the new state and the new job and new people, but the words bounce around in my skull and take on the tone of people from my past.

**I read a story once about a girl who took her skeletons with her when she moved because she had read a story once about a girl who had tried to bury her skeletons in the park but in shoveling dirt over their bones had turned to stone. The girl that took her skeletons with her couldn't find a big enough box to put them all in and so had to ask the undertaker—yes, I'm being serious—to use a box that he got coffins shipped to him in, and it turned out that that box worked. The skeletons, at least in the story, weren't happy about being put into a box that once held something that holds dead things.*

The Nature of Her Leaving

her name felt funny and special in my mouth

On a hot summer day made hazy by time lapsed, Nathia pulled up to our house for her first time working with me. I was three years old. I don't remember much about her, beyond how her name felt funny and special in my mouth.

At that time, because of my age, the service I received was called "respite," as in, giving parents of disabled kids "respite" from taking care of them. This word didn't have a definition in my mind until I was older, or if it did, it was associated with high school, maybe college-aged girls coming over to hang out with me and help me. I never connected it with this idea of taking a break until much later, when I was teetering on the edge of young adulthood and frustrated autonomy. "We say it's called respite because it's giving her a break from us," my mom would say when we interviewed new helpers. I'd grow out of being able to receive respite, but other labels would replace this one: consumer directed attendant care, supported community living, Vocational Rehabilitation—all different terms for essentially the same thing, a personal care assistant to act as my arms and legs. The titles changed; the job didn't.

The other consistent factor: Nathia—and every other helper to come after her—left.

visions of skeletons climbing out of my closet

I'm twenty-five and I'm leaving Kansas. It's the end of summer 2020 and

I'm going back home to Iowa to do my final year of grad school remotely, living with my parents and primarily being cared for by them, because of the pandemic. The deep sadness I felt at the beginning of the pandemic has not gone away, although it has slowly been joined by an anger and a hurt and a fear that *is* new to me. The more time goes on and the more it becomes apparent that people who do not believe themselves to be high risk will refuse to sacrifice their comfort for the lives of others, the more these emotions grow.

Two years ago, likely to the day, I left Iowa City where I'd lived independently (that is, without my parents) for five years. The week that I left, I had visions of skeletons climbing out of my closet, and refusing to stay behind as I left the town I had learned to call home. Amidst the chaos of packing up my apartment in Kansas—I'm forced to sit and watch and do nothing as my parents take down and pack up the pieces of my life I have built and sculpted here—my mind keeps circling back to two years ago. I'd experienced the dissociation of leaving Iowa City as looking out at the world from behind a wall that's behind your eyes. There is a double layer of removal from reality, two steps back.

we say it's a choice

At the end of my freshman year of undergrad, I was in the middle of telling one of my helpers I didn't think it'd be a good idea for her to continue working for me the following year when the fire alarms in my dorm went off. Amidst my churning stomach and progressing state of numbness, we made our way to the lobby, where we waited for the all-clear. She sat on one of those generic looking couches that college dormitory lobbies have, and warned me against burning bridges—the implication being, of course, that as someone who needs others to keep me alive, I risked losing a lifeline I had, despite the fact that I dreaded each shift she worked and was made to feel guilty for asking for her help.

I don't fully understand the desperate irony of this situation until six years later, one morning while listening to "Bridge on Fire," a song by folk-rock duo Shovels & Rope, and I'm reminded of the particular cruelty of telling someone you've mistreated that they need you. It's the end of the first week of classes of my final year of grad school, and my mom is helping me shower. We're both getting used to the forced reality that my parents and I will need to lower our level of required safety precautions for potential helpers if we're going to find people to help me while I'm home. There's no way of knowing for sure, but we decide that one potential helper is probably safe, as safe as we're going to get—one in-person class, but only four students, all masked and spaced out. Since he's in nursing school, he'll start clinicals at the hospital the fifth week of the semester. My parents and I weigh the risks. We say it's a choice, as in *we have no other choice.* I need helpers in order to live, and I likely won't live if I contract the virus.

In the lobby of my college dorm: the lights were bright and white and curved into misshapen stars through the pools of water forming in my eyes. The fact that I never actually let these tears spill over onto my cheeks throughout this entire exchange baffles me now. I don't know whether to be impressed with my younger self for "keeping it together," or ache with the knowledge that I didn't feel safe enough to cry in front of this particular helper, to show her, fully, how beaten down she made me feel.

The basis of abuse is control: the abuser has control of the person they are abusing, and they maintain that control through manipulation, and fear, and wearing away at the victim's self-esteem. Sometimes this means taking advantage of someone's naivete and asserting one's dominance by showing that the other person's body can still feel pleasure even if they have said they don't want it, that they want out. Sometimes this means not informing someone fully of what they are about to get into because it is clear they don't have enough understanding of the subject to question the other person. Sometimes this is not sexual at all, but merely a manipulation of someone who is dependent on their abuser, and so the abuser knows that they will get away with it.

Sometimes, it's like the story Fi wrote when we were both in Ireland, about the girl whose grandfather leaves her and her wheelchair out in the sun for too long, making the cast on her leg melt and burn her skin.

Rates of abuse of disabled women are twice as high as non-disabled women. Disabled men are twice as likely to be sexually abused than non-disabled men. Thirty-three percent of abusers are acquaintances, 33 percent are family members, and 25 percent are hired caregivers. But considering that many disabled people rely on caretaking by someone else, whether they're officially hired or not, the likelihood of the abuser being someone the disabled person is reliant on doesn't necessarily fit these statistics.

Caretaking and care*giving*. What, exactly, do the shape of these words hold?

"Care practice . . . requires the collaboration of both bodies on multiple levels," disability studies scholar Akemi Nishida writes. "A process which twirls both bodies beyond the boundaries of their skin." In her book *Care Work: Dreaming Disability Justice,* Leah Lakshmi Piepzna-Samarasinha proposes an the idea of "care webs," similar to what is talked about in Nishida's piece: a re-situating of the caree/carer relationship, so that they are not seen as roles pitted against one another, or even two identities positioned at opposite ends of a spectrum. This is a marvelous and even revolutionary understanding of the unique dynamic that occurs between someone who needs help and someone who gives help: it can be a symbiotic, mutual aid scenario. Disabled people have, after all, *Crip magic,* knowledge and skills we have perfected because of our interdependent lives. But still—I want a world like Lakshmi Piepzna-Samarasinha's friend envisions and tells her about: a world in which "I don't ever want to depend on being liked or loved by the community for the right to shit in my toilet when I want to."

It wasn't until I read a definition of emotional abuse that I could confront what had happened to me my freshman year of college with one of my helpers. Surely a part of me knew that something was wrong with the relationship all along—the part of me that turned my stomach into knots before her shift, perhaps. But sometimes, the mind refuses to listen to the body.

trying to lick the blood from my cuts

Once I found the words for emotional abuse, the way that helper interacted with me started to make sense. Experiences started to connect with words, words started to connect with meaning. When I told E. one afternoon while we sat in a dark bar, her sipping a beer, me taking a shot of Jameson because I wanted to impress her, she was outraged. *Oh, she's reacting how she should be reacting,* I registered through the cloud of whiskey. But then, being upset about your friend being manipulated and emotionally abused is part and parcel to friendship. It is perhaps no more reason to be attracted to someone than knowing they don't litter—basic, common good. Still, attraction is rarely logical. It rarely stops to analyze the fact that sometimes it burns for wickedness, and sometimes it burns for decency.

E. and I did not end well. I reacted to her eventual rejection like a wounded animal, hurt, seething, trying to lick the blood from my cuts. My mom was worried because I'd called her crying, nights in a row, refusing to explain why I was so upset. This worry pained me more than the fear of coming out to my parents, so one night I told them, feeling like I was going to throw up, and because I am lucky and privileged and have parents who just seem to get it, they said *rejection sucks, hurting hurts, we love you*, and I had one less wound to try to sew up on my own.

a bomb on the verge of going off

I have driven home to Iowa from Lawrence, Kansas, three times since March 2020. Once, for the spring break of my second year of grad school, before the pandemic fully hit. Once, at the beginning of June, after receiving my most recent injection of Spinraza at the hospital in Kansas City. And once, again, now. In many ways, I feel as if I am fleeing a bomb on the verge of going off—I leave Lawrence the week before classes start, just as the young college kids begin to take over, with their haphazard mask wearing and affinity for distances less than six feet.

"I'm so glad your time in Lawrence this time has been better than when you were here before," one of my helpers who was able to isolate for a short time tells me. She was my very first helper when I moved to Kansas, and I know I can rely on her like a rock. When I thank her for isolating so that she can help me and I can come back to Kansas for a spell, she shrugs. "It's not like I'm not getting anything out of it, either," she says. "Working long shifts for these two and a half weeks will pay for my new car. And it's not like I hate hanging out with you." I laugh.

Now, we're spooning ice cream into our mouths for dinner, one of those beautiful choices that living in my own apartment affords me. Over the course of these two and a half weeks—the length of time I am able to stay in Lawrence before returning home—I get the world's best ice cream, Sylas and Maddy's, for takeout over and over and over. And my helper is right: This time is so, so much better.

When I came to Lawrence at the beginning of the summer after being home for two months, I was greeted by park meetups with friends, being able to spend all day with my cat, my own apartment, and O., the girl I had fallen for, telling me she had unexpectedly met someone new. You shouldn't fall in love in the middle of a pandemic, especially with a girl who is exposed to many people every day, especially if you have shitty lungs, especially if this girl can't figure out how to commit to someone she cannot kiss.

How hard I tried to stay. My balcony became a home to plant clippings and dirt, green shoots I thought I could remove from their original homes to propagate for myself: the clover, the chamomile look alike that was actually prairie fleabane, the morning glory. It was something I could not let go of, the stubborn desire to see their lives through. And yet, trying to coax life from tendrils of plant clippings that you yourself snipped with scissors is a delicate process. I ended up pressing many of these leaves and flowers in *The Wake Forest Book of Irish Women's Poetry,* the tome which carried the mermaids. The pressed clippings were beautiful, but they weren't what I wanted, and because of this they broke my heart. This time in Lawrence was meant to be a getaway, as much of a vacation as I could afford amidst the apocalypse I felt our world becoming. "I just don't want to be here," I cried to my mom one night over the phone. "I want to come home." But I did stay. I stayed till my injection, scheduled for June 1 at University of Kansas Med Center in Kansas City.

The hospital had put in place new policies under COVID-19 that say I must be unaccompanied when I come for this injection. A friend of mine with the same disease as I have is able to do this no problem.

Physically, I'm weaker than my friend. I suppose this translates to my disease being more progressed than hers. I need much more assistance being transferred to the bed, being made comfortable, being readjusted throughout the waiting period.

More than that—each injection (they have to occur every four months) has grown increasingly emotionally taxing for me. I got my first injection of Spinraza in November 2018. When I am wheeled back to the room in which they perform the procedure, I immediately register the blank-faced men in scrubs and masks. It's as if I am noticing this detail from a distance. In past writing on the spinal fusion surgery I had when I was eight, I described the blank-faced men in the operating room. It's not *eerily* similar, because of course there is nothing surprising about this sight.

It happens something like this: each book you read is informed by the books you've consumed in the past, each poem you write built from the words you spilled previously, and suddenly I'm no longer panicking solely in the operating room when the shot of Lidocaine burns my side but in the room where I am sent to wait, on a bed, hooked up to the heart monitor that somehow refuses to betray the wild, galloping numbness spreading inside of me.

"Just explain you need help," my mom said. "Tell them you need someone with you, and that I'll suit up and can wear gloves and a face shield if they want." This possibility didn't even occur to me until she mentioned it. The doctor agreed. I can have someone with me to help with transfers. We decided on my mom. My dad will have to wait it out.

The night before, my mom helped me shower in my apartment in Lawrence. I break down crying as hot water hits my body, still reeling from the breakup. "When I was with A., I just assumed she would come to one of my injections," I eventually told my mom, referring to my first girlfriend. "And then there was Moon-Hair Girl, and she was going to come for an injection, but of course that never happened. And now this."

Before I am taken back for the spinal injection that morning, I wait with my mom in the cove I've been assigned. I'm lying in a bed, IV prepped and ready to receive the drugs which will lightly sedate me. She is sitting in a chair beside the bed.

"I know Dad wishes he could be here," she says, and unwittingly I start to cry. "It's okay," my mom says, rubbing my hand. "There are so many people with you right now, even if it doesn't feel like it. It's okay."

I had met O. in a cemetery, days before driving back to Kansas for my injection. Being in her presence made my body thrum. "You can't tell I'm smiling behind this mask," she had said, "except for the ways my eyes crinkle." And they crinkled a lot. Near the end of our hangout, as my stomach was beginning to growl with hunger, O. told me she would take off work to quarantine and then come see me in Lawrence. Somehow, among all the green things growing, she found a four-leaf clover and gave it to me. A week later, in my apartment in Kansas, I had my helper page through Anna Tsing's *The Mushroom at the End of the World* to find where I had pressed the four-leaf clover and thrown the now-dead clover in the trash. This particular flavor of abandonment is not one I am equipped to stomach.

why didn't i trust her?

Haley came from Iowa for my very first injection. Haley was the roommate of one of my helpers my freshman year of undergrad, and by the end of that first year, I'd hired her on. She's a year older than me, which meant she graduated when I was a junior, something that filled me with unending spirals of dread. By this point, I had had over eighty helpers come into my life:

HELPERS, A LIST

Nathia, Amber, Logan, Lacey, Lisa, Caitlin, Estee, Ioana, Madison, Elly, Haley, Bailey, Carissa, Hannah, Haven, Connie, Sarah, Brittany, Katie, Heidy, Karen, Karen, Chessa, Jessica, Claire, Danielle, Mary, Kali, Delaney, Lorin, Lauren, Lauren, Lexi, Hope, Maddy, Jacy, Katie, Taylor, Lexi, Madeline, Marlee, Meghan, Megan, Courtney, Aaron, Erin, Geo, Megan, Colby, Cole, Claire, Maritza, Riley, Emma, Raeme, Nicole, Nicole, Laura, Lara, Megan, Hayden, Bethany, Sierra, Sarah, Abbey, Alex, Alicia, Naomi, Amanda, Anna, Natalie, Ashley, Nicole,

Paige, Pauline, Rachel, Shellie, Steph, Susan, Yeyoung, Shillan, Audrey, Zipporah, Brook, Candi, Tina, Teena, Chilpa

I maintained friendships with some helpers after they left, but it's not possible to sustain relationships with that many people on the same level of closeness I had while they were helping me.

"Ok, but we're going to stay in each other's lives, right?" became a constant litany of mine when Haley was working, during those final months of her senior year. She always assured me, usually with a hint of exasperation, that we would, of course, remain best friends. Why didn't I trust her?

Haley's last shift ended with her taking me to my undergrad essay workshop, which E. was also in. We hugged in the hallway, took a selfie, and tried very hard not to cry. After she got me set up at my desk with my notebook and pen and water bottle, Haley left, and I sat in a classroom with the first girl I realized I had feelings for, feeling myself shrink farther and farther inside of myself as the professor welcomed us to our last day. It was textbook dissociation, and it felt similar to the weight being pressed down around me that night, years before, when my helper warned me against burning bridges as the fire alarms blared around us.

we must do the things we think we cannot do

Before Haley graduated, before I fell for our mutual friend who wrote pieces about the ephemerality of fire and the things she would burn on the banks of the Iowa River, before I spent mornings during a pandemic writing prayers to our backyard meadow, I had to tell a certain helper that she wasn't coming back to work for me the following year, because she had done such a masterful job of making me believe that the fault of our shaky relationship lay within me, and so, amidst the piercing of the fire alarms and the flashing of the lights, I had agreed to let her stay.

Another friend made me realize how horrible of an idea this was, and I soon made plans to tell this helper that continuing work would not be a good idea. I sat in class before her last shift, feeling sick to my stomach and reciting Eleanor Roosevelt's *We must do the things we think we cannot do* over and over in my mind, a line I would learn, years later, is also a favorite of my mom and grandma. The plan was that I would tell her at the beginning of her shift, right before we went to the dining hall for supper, where my friends would meet us. My friends were to be a buffer, a way to make sure I wasn't alone with her for too long after I broke the news, a way to make sure I felt safe.

I wasn't used to cutting people out of my life. I'm still not. My survival depends upon other people and their help.

One night, years and years later, I'm lying in bed in Iowa in the middle of a pandemic and think, *My God, of course. I was eight years old and she left me.*

the nature of her leaving

For every photograph of me as a child making silly faces or piling my hair with soap bubbles, there is one of me looking intently into the camera, mouth pursed somewhere between a scowl and a look of skepticism. I don't know the source of these expressions, only that having them captured on film makes it easier for me to contextualize the pieces from my spinal fusion surgery that I don't remember, a surgery that took place at the University of Iowa Hospitals and Clinics in Iowa City years before I would move there for college and rebuild my perception of the town, carefully covering it in new memories.

At some point, between being wheeled back to the operating room and falling asleep, the hysterical eight-year-old me was told by my mom that everything was going to be okay. "No, it won't," I'd said. And then the mask with anesthesia was placed on my face, and everything went dark, and she left.

the thing about bridges

The thing about bridges. Well, the thing about bridges is that—The thing about bridges is that they're primarily built for a certain type of travel, and thus by default a certain type of body. Of course they make things possible. That is, you could argue, the point of bridges.

or it can drown you

I'm sitting outside on our back deck in Iowa, facing the meadow that makes up a good portion of our backyard, and I'm listening to two birds calling at each other from different ends of the meadow. This week has been a week of rain, and as such, partnered with the Midwest derecho, the plants in the meadow are looking pretty beaten down.

"I love hot water," I told my helper in the shower that morning.

"Water is the stuff of life!" he said. "Well, or it can drown you."

I don't know if what I experienced as an eight-year-old constitutes our clinical definitions of trauma. Nor do I know if the statistic of 20 percent of individuals who have undergone spinal fusion surgery being later diagnosed with PTSD applies to me. My therapist thinks it does, but at times I find myself hesitant to believe what she tells me, just as I am often hesitant to believe that people are attracted to and interested in me.

What I do know is that there are moments of departure, forceful and violent and ripping, that leave me no longer in my body. If I do remain in my body during these instances, I am somehow desperate to find ways of escape. Isn't the fact that, after a breakup, I throw up morning after morning, evidence of me trying to leave myself?

In the meadow, the coneflowers have largely turned black, perhaps burned by the oppressive sun, which has been a constant in between storms. But also, the baby hummingbirds have hatched and left the nest, and so when I am sitting outside, trying to write, faced with the meadow, I am sometimes granted a low buzz, a thrum, the sound of a hummingbird fluttering by to dip its long beak into our feeders. I am choosing to take this as a sign of hope. But then, a friend from undergrad tells me over FaceTime that she's pregnant, and although I am dancing and singing with excitement over video, there's also the nagging thought, wriggling its way into the back of my mind: What sort of world will her child be born into? Will they be able to be greeted by their relatives? Hugged by her friends?

Months later, I have a dream that I am in my shower chair, my body on the brink of sliding out of it, falling onto the floor. The same helper who's said water is the stuff of life that also can drown you is in the same tiled room as I am, but ignores my cries for help. I wake up before I hit the ground.

Six Ways in Which the Body Becomes Narrative

I. THE BODY AS ABSORBER

When we first moved into our current house, my dad insisted that before we spent money on decorations or unnecessary furniture, we plant trees in our yard, so that (as I would learn years later from my mom) our trees would be fully grown sooner.

I was two years old then, nearly three. There's a memory I have that has somehow burned its way into the back of my mind from the morning of our move: I'm wearing pink Minnie Mouse pajamas in our old house, and I must have been sick or nervous or both because I threw up my breakfast onto my pajamas and it was an alarmingly bright orange color, set off by the bright pink of my PJs. At some point during my childhood, my brother, who's three years older than me, told me that "technicolor" means vomit. Despite my intense skepticism of just about everything, this made sense to me, and so I believed him.

Whether this particular moment of throwing up was due to nerves or not, I'm prone to think that surely anxiety had *something* to do with it, because twenty-three years later I still hold my fears in my stomach, still absorb the stressors from the world into my body, and during especially horrible bouts of anxiety, puke.

We're in the middle of a global pandemic and I'm home in Iowa, at the house we moved into the morning of my vibrant display of nervousness, the house with the trees which are, in fact, full grown, and I am sitting outside in the meadow my dad has transformed our backyard into, my wheelchair (and thus, my body) positioned next to the coneflowers and the milkweed and the black-eyed Susans. As I let the sun press its heat down onto my skin, I realize that I can pull my top lip in between my teeth and chew on it until a swollen bump forms over which I can run my tongue for the rest of the day. This constant reminder of what I can do to my body is comforting, although I know it shouldn't be.

When I was in middle school, I'd pick the dry skin off my lips till they bled. I didn't realize why I did this—treated my body as a stress ball—just that I did. These were also some of the worst years of my depression and anxiety, before I had finally worked up the courage to tell my mom I needed help and was taken to a psychologist who promptly diagnosed me. The part of me which finally asked for help is the part of me which knows not to get too attached to the feeling of bruising my own mouth, that it's a temporary distraction at best.

Earlier that day, before I sat in our meadow and caused the inside of my lip to swell by worrying it with my teeth, my helper tells me he'll be doing a blood drive for students at his college, and that he'll be going to campus as soon as he leaves here. He started his clinicals at the hospital two weeks ago, meaning he's around unmasked patients once a week, but when he's there, he's at least in full PPE. Still, he tells me about his weekend trip to the mall to get soap at Bath and Body Works and laments the many people he saw not wearing masks. He tells me he's flying home to the West Coast the last week of October, and I eventually work up the nerve to tell him that he'll have to wait, then, before coming back to work with me. "We can try that," he had said, "but just so you know, I am following all of the proper safety guidelines, and not to throw you under the bus, but I need hours, or I am going to have to start looking for another job." *Not to throw you under the bus.*

Throughout this whole conversation, he's sitting on the bean bag in my bedroom, and I'm perched in my wheelchair. In this context, I'm higher than him—a rare scenario when he's six feet tall and usually towers above me, even when I'm in my tall shower chair, which I brought home from Kansas for him to use. But the height difference in this moment doesn't do a whole lot, although it is a fact I am keenly aware of, just as I am keenly aware of the different definitions of "proper safety guidelines" that people have, and that, for him, this does not include the CDC suggestion to quarantine after travel, especially air travel. I am equally aware of the way my skin has gotten clammy, another sign from my body that I'm in a situation causing me anxiety. I've learned to look for these signs from my body, because the pandemic has effectively warped my understanding of fear into something language fails.

Last fall, in a class on representations of trauma in literature, a woman in my program used the word "worry" to describe the constant lip biting her protagonist does, until there is a permanent bruise on their mouth, a physical signifier of trauma. "Worry" feels right to me, as a response to all of this, just like the swollen lip bump feels right, until it doesn't.

II. THE BODY AS POLITICAL CURRENCY

Jayne Mattingly, a chronically ill and disabled therapist, wrote in a January 2022 opinion piece for NBC News that she is tired of feeling like chronically ill individuals, herself included, are being used as political pawns in the COVID-19 pandemic. Mattingly's piece was written in response to the CDC Director's comments that it is "encouraging" that the majority of deaths from the Omicron variant were of people with underlying conditions, and the ways this comment was used by people who were anti-mask or anti-vax to support their arguments. "I am still at risk of getting extremely sick or dying, and that's met with a lot of resistance and shoulder-shrugging on both sides of the aisle," Mattingly writes.

I was so hopeful when Biden was finally declared the winner of the 2020 election, because of his pandemic response plan. But as time went on, I felt disappointment after disappointment related to his administration's handling of COVID. The rollout of vaccines, the flip-flopping on mask wearing—it all felt as if his goal was to not end the pandemic, but to move on. To make it "safe enough" for "healthy" people, and to forget that protecting immuno-compromised people is very well the only way to effectively end the pandemic, as explained in an NPR article: Because studies have shown that the COVID vaccines are less effective on those with compromised immune systems to begin with, it is probable that new variants of the virus can form and take root in the bodies of these individuals. Prioritizing their safety, instead of, say, economic capital and others' desire to go to a bar, party, wedding, etc., is a key component of ending COVID-19. Imagine that.

When a record number of delegates with disclosed disabilities attended the Democratic National Convention in 2016, I believed we were moving forward. When disability advocate Anastasia Somoza spoke at the DNC and then toured with the Hillary for America campaign, I believed we were moving forward. When Biden had a pandemic response plan and then was officially inaugurated into the White House, I believed we were moving forward. We were, and we are. These accomplishments are no small things. Compared to options presented by the major opposing political party (let alone by Biden's forerunner), they are huge. But they can be better, and our commitment to holistically improving the lived experiences of disabled people must go beyond lip service. We shouldn't mark our progress by *how bad it could be,* but by *how much further we can go.* I don't just mean this in relation to politics. I mean a societal, cultural interrogation of how we turn people and their bodies and their minds into stories, so a point can be proven. I mean conscious and careful attention to how we turn bodies into political currency.

In 2016, fourteen-year-old Jerika Bolen, who also had SMA, chose to end her own life, citing immense amounts of chronic pain from numerous surgeries she had throughout her life. Jerika's choice left me sobbing in my bed, but the media coverage of Jerika's choice and the "last dance" that was being held in her honor made me sick—as someone with SMA who has been suicidal, but also as a writer.

At that time, I was about to start my final year of undergrad majoring in English and Journalism, and wrote a piece for *Disability Visibility Project* about how the inherently ableist news articles that were covering this were harmful to not just other disabled individuals, who would now see ending one's life as a laudable choice, but also to non-disabled individuals, who would now have narratives that reinforced the belief that disabled lives are not worth living. *This story isn't about her decision*, I had written in my piece. And it wasn't, but now it is.

When the news broke of Jerika's decision to end her own life, and of the "last dance" that would be held for her, the disability community that I'm a part of began letter writing campaigns discussing how we love our lives as disabled individuals and talking on social media about how

SMA doesn't cause pain, that there were other options, like counseling for mental health and pain management alternatives.

But also—during the long months of the pandemic, another friend with SMA has surgery to hopefully alleviate ongoing pain, and while the procedure goes well, her pain does not go away.

Writers and scholars and other disabled individuals have theorized that doctors' rejection of patients' symptoms can be a form of trauma, and that such experiences may eventually cause someone to question their own bodily experiences, and thus their own grip on reality. Medical gaslighting, with causes so insidious they are barely recognizable. And this is all eerily similar—too similar—to what so many of us were doing in the weeks prior to Jerika's last dance and death.

Jerika was black and queer—she would be bringing her girlfriend to the last dance—two facets of her identity that I and others failed to take into account in 2016. Pain and symptoms of illness from women, particularly women of color, have historically been met with denial from doctors. Rebecca Wanzo's work, for example, has shown that African Americans are undertreated for pain, likely because healthcare professionals may believe that the pain someone is describing is not as bad as they say it is. This suffering, then, can easily result in African Americans—especially African American women—being less likely to seek pain management and routine care from doctors.

I want to be able to continue to interrogate the systems that put Jerika in this position in the first place, and the narratives that framed her death as the only option. I want to be able to do all of this without erasing her own bodily experience, because even though Jerika and I shared a genetic condition there was still the ultimate unknowability of her trauma, the ultimate unknowability of her experience.

I want people's deaths—and their lives—to not be in vain while at the same time being conscious to not force stories on them which squelch out their complicated, messy humanity. I don't want us to turn away from the truth of a situation. I want a different kind of story.

III. THE BODY AS DISPOSABLE

And so, in some rivers, the great salmon run—scaly bodies returning from the ocean to gravel beds to mate and lay eggs, after which they will die. But the rivers don't teem with wild salmon the way they used to, their numbers dwindling from overharvesting and habitat destruction in the rivers and the oceans. It's not that there aren't any wild salmon anymore, it's that our greed and complacency as humans has made them nearly exotic. This is, please understand, not a metaphor.

On a FaceTime date with O., nearly a year ago now, she tells me about the research she has started to do while revising her grad school thesis, and how it has been shown that mere exposure to people who are different from us can lead to increased levels of acceptance of these people and these differences. "Just think how applicable this is to right now," she tells me excitedly, in reference to the shelter in place orders and work being moved to remote in lieu of the pandemic. "The sheltering in place is going to lead to less exposure of diverse people, which will then in turn impact people's perceptions and acceptance of them."

"Yes," I say, "but people still need to be staying home."

O. exhales. "I know, Hannah, I know."

Ugly Laws, 2021: A resurgence of the ordinances imposed throughout various US cities that made it illegal for "unsightly" individuals ("diseased, maimed, mutilated, or deformed," as stated in an 1867 ordinance in San Francisco) to be seen in public, ordinances which were not repealed in some cities *until 1974*, except now, these are never cemented into law, only permeate through our society, moving from one group of people en masse to the next, its own contagion.

The Ugly Laws were meant to target various groups of people, some of them overlapping: people with visible physical differences, unhoused individuals, and those in poverty. If you appeared in public anytime from 1876 to 1974 and were somehow "unsightly or disgusting" (as stated in the Chicago City Code of 1881), you could be arrested, as Arthur Honeyman was in Portland, Oregon, in 1971. He and his deaf friend, Richard Pimental, were at a pancake house trying to eat pancakes for Art's birthday, and their waitress said she would call the police on "the most disgusting looking person" she'd seen in her life. They told her to call the police. The ruling judge found them guilty of breaking an Ugly Law. Out of sight, out of mind, hopefully out of future generations.

Natural selection, survival of the fittest, it's simply evolution except when orchestrated by the hands of humans, targeting other humans. Then, we call it eugenics, and think of the forced sterilization of over 64,000 people in the United States from 1907 to 1963, intentionally targeting people of color, people who were poor, and people with all types of disabilities. Bodies as disposable then, bodies as disposable now.

It's a sticky thing, now—high-risk individuals, "the undesirables," go out in public and aren't punished, exactly, except with the possible contraction of a virus that can kill us. So, we stay inside, and the longer we stay inside, the farther we're removed from public consciousness. I wasn't willing to risk exposure to a virus that could easily kill me through a kiss, which meant I wasn't willing to risk exposure to a virus that could easily kill me through physical intimacy, which meant, really, that I wasn't willing to risk my life. Never would I have predicted how my own desire to survive—how the disability community's desire to survive—would be weaponized against us.

Utah, October 2020, six months after my grandma's best friend Jolly dies: hospitals prepare to ration care as COVID-19 cases surge. Translation: In Utah, in October, hospitals prepare to say "your life isn't valuable enough as someone with your type of body to allow you admittance to our beds." Under Utah's rationing criteria, patients in the ICU whose health is continuing to decline would get removed from the hospital and thus removed from care first. This could, then, theoretically include me. If there are cases where the condition of two patients seem on equal footing, the younger patient would get to stay, because, as *The Salt Lake Tribune* reports, "older patients are more likely to die." This could, then, theoretically include my grandparents.

When I feel up to it, which really means when I can't ignore the urge any longer, I write Instagram and Facebook posts trying to make sense of the continual disregard of disabled people's lives, of my friends' lives, of my life. I learn, in these moments, that a like on social media, even a comment of support, does not equal true understanding, as I continue to see friends and family members posting about parties, about weddings, about bars, about football games.

In Iowa, 42 percent of those who died from COVID as of January 2021 were residents of nursing homes such as the Iowa Veterans Home. This isn't confined to Iowa: It's reported nationwide that COVID deaths disproportionately occur in long-term care facilities, something which all experts agree is a crime. The implication of this, though, that those living in long-term care facilities are already essentially quarantined, and thus that the virus is being brought in by staff and visitors, isn't something the news talks about, although it's a realization that stirs a cauldron of grief and rage inside me. When I write a Facebook post about this, an old teacher from my high school comments that we can't expect people to stay in their bubbles outside of work, and I'm left thinking, *But can't we? Can't we and shouldn't we be expecting more from people when there are lives on the line?*

After all, there's a difference between individuals who work in long-term care facilities needing to work multiple jobs, as these jobs pay very low (as discussed in coverage of this), and being exposed this way, versus selfish recklessness: attending large gatherings, not wearing masks when seeing new people or going out to bars and restaurants and parties and football games. When Iowa begins to vaccinate healthcare workers, including those who work in long-term care facilities, more than 40 percent of workers at the Iowa Veterans Home refuse to be vaccinated.

In the fall, my dad's brother calls to ask if he can drop off wild cod, salmon, and halibut he caught on a recent fishing trip to Alaska, on his way to a football game in Ames, a town thirty miles north of us, which happens to be COVID hotspot. My uncle and his family live three hours east of us, are staunchly Catholic, and voted for Trump in 2016. Now, four years later, they have changed. "We need to get the Cheeto out," my uncle tells my dad over the phone, and I wonder, again, about the contradictions living within us all.

Disability rights lawyer, activist, and writer Harriet McBryde Johnson tells of her experience with outwardly polite eugenicist Peter Singer in "Unspeakable Conversations," an essay I stumbled upon my freshman year of college and have since read again and again. Singer, a renowned moral philosopher perhaps most famous for his progressive ideas on animal liberation, believes strongly that disabled babies should not be born, and that we should be allowed to kill disabled babies at birth (see: eugenics). The unspeakable conversation, then, is that which Harriet McBryde Johnson has at Princeton University, with Singer and his class. Johnson is confounded by the way he treats her like a human being and like an adult—something she is not used to from the majority of people she interacts with as a visibly disabled wheelchair user.

Johnson wrestles with Singer's behavior alongside the knowledge that he believes she should have been killed at birth, and by the end, reaches this conclusion: "If I define Singer's kind of disability prejudice as an ultimate evil, and him as a monster, then I must so define all who believe disabled lives are inherently worse off or that a life without a certain kind of consciousness lacks value." And, Johnson understands, this definition reaches to many people she interacts with daily, including some of her family members and many of her nondisabled friends.

I used to be able to see this conclusion as a product of Johnson's self-described Southern niceness (which is, of course, a loaded term)—to not view Singer as a monster, surely, is naive. But my reality has changed, and with it, my perspective: Johnson's ending is not naive, it is what she has to do to survive. If she were to assign Peter Singer to this category of monster, she'd also have to relegate people in her life to this category, something she is not able to do, not because she doesn't want to, but because she relies on others to keep her alive—as we all do, but as is especially apparent in the disability community. I need more than physical assistance to keep me alive: I need people who care about me and my community, and I need the existence of hope. I can't live in a world surrounded by people I believe are monsters, and this has never been more clear to me than now, in the middle of a pandemic.

How do you do it? I text my friend, Jess, who lives in Canada and has an undiagnosed form of Muscular Dystrophy. Jess is also extremely high risk due to compromised lungs. *How do you continue relationships with people who keep showing that they don't care?*

Oh friend, I know, she writes back. *It's so hard.*

I can't just cut people out of my life. I can't do that.

Oh, I can't either. I've just had to distance myself from people for a while.

But this is also hard for me, because I don't like creating boundaries without communicating them first. The battle to hold space in my mind for people I love who are participating in activities that put my community at risk is exhausting, but I don't know, yet, any other way.

Until: a year into the pandemic, a friend tells me she is regularly attending large parties with (clearly) unmasked individuals, and, while I sit in my childhood bedroom and cry silent, angry tears at this new wound, I experience something akin to what feminist theorist Sara Ahmed calls the "feminist snap," when the smiling and nodding and pretending not to be bothered by something will no longer do.

This is a "Crip snap," then: a year into the pandemic, and I am no longer willing to compromise my need for friends who stick up for me and my community when it matters most. When I realize this, I am sitting in front of my bedroom window, looking out at Iowa's incessant snow of that winter. It is clear, then, as clear as the heaps upon heaps of whiteness covering our neighborhood: *you cannot love me and care about me and claim to support me while also participating in activities which have clearly been shown to spread a virus that is killing people like me.* For the past year, I witnessed people simply looking the other way, and I am suddenly refusing to accept this anymore.

I realize, then, that if I let this slide in my friendships with people who do not view themselves as high risk, I am not only doing a disservice to the authenticity of that relationship, but I am also not doing right by my other disabled and high-risk friends who are in the same position as I am. I know this same conclusion doesn't feel right for everyone, or even that everyone in my position is able to do this—asking for accountability from someone can be fraught and complicated if the person you are asking accountability from is someone you rely on to keep you alive. But at this point, I know no other way forward.

Later that night, I will cry into my mom's shirt, her arms around me. I don't know how to make sense of this new wound beyond baring it for someone to see, pointing to the ache and saying, *it hurts, it hurts, it hurts. When will it stop hurting?*

"I'm so sick of it," I sobbed. "I'm just so, so sick of it."

After the breakup, the image of O. kissing another girl—a girl whose legs wrap around O. in a way mine never could, a kiss immortalized on Instagram and Facebook—sears itself into my mind, and I'm left wondering what *I can't commit to anything or anyone right now* means. And then, also, in June of 2020 in *The New York Times* magazine: "Is It OK to Dump Him Because of His Medical Condition?"—an advice column, can you believe it (you can't, but I can)? And although the columnist responded that it's decidedly *not* okay to do this, the presence of this question still broke me.

In the nights following the photo and the advice column, I sink into a darkness so complete—a darkness that steals light from everything in its reach—that I begin to see myself through the lens of the very worst of what the pandemic has laid bare about our society: I'm not worthy, my life doesn't matter, self-harm isn't really such a bad idea because who I am as a disabled woman isn't a way of being that the world actually cares about.

The deep well of depression I fell into was not created solely by the breakup or even the way the breakup played out; yes, it hurt, but I had been through such things before, and although they left me severely depressed and wanting to crawl out of my own skin, I hadn't thought of self-harming or even flirted with suicidal thoughts for years. My reality had changed, though. This breakup happened within the context of a pandemic that left some people merely mourning the loss of travel plans while others drafted their wills. What I kept coming back to, what I held onto like a branch in the river to keep myself from drowning, what saved me: at the end of the day, I wanted to survive by not contracting COVID, and this was a good thing; wanting to live was a good thing.

The pandemic rages on. I'm still unable to extend the definition of *monster* to those in my life who see disability as lacking value, because, like disabled Mestiza writer Naomi Ortiz says in her book *Sustaining Spirit,* "I need to believe that change is possible," even if I don't witness it. There are millions of people who would agree that Peter Singer's beliefs regarding disabled babies are horrific. But so what? If these people are also participating in activities clearly linked to spreading a virus that's killing sick and disabled people, where is their line of *enough is enough*? In some ways, I'd rather deal with the Peter Singers, because their belittling of my life is out in the open, their violence toward myself and my community not hidden behind *I love you* and *of course I care about you*.

And yet, here is the eternal conundrum: if I ended relationships with every person who demonstrated their inherent devaluing of disabled life over the past two years, I would have very few people left in my life. Is this a tragedy, or just reality? Perhaps it's both. But I also know that cutting myself off from people I love who have shown me they don't understand my lived reality as a high-risk, disabled woman living during a pandemic feels like admitting defeat to a culture that has shown time and time again it would be more convenient if I could just stay shut inside, away from society. What I can do, though, is no longer pour energy into relationships that I feel silenced in. And in this action, too, I am honoring my desire to live.

When we attempt to grill the wild salmon for Thanksgiving in the winter cold, we fumble in the early dark of the evening, and the fish is left dry, its body, a body reliant on the sea, shriveled by the flames of our making.

IV. THE BODY AS REPRESSED EMOTION / THE BODY AS VOLCANO / THE BODY AS A DRAIN ON THE SYSTEM

In the winter, during the eleventh month of the pandemic, I force myself to look beyond the next month. When I am fully vaccinated, and my helpers are fully vaccinated, it is my hope and plan to go back to Kansas. I will defend my thesis in May, I will graduate, I will have the summer in Kansas with my friends before . . . what?

Since I first moved away from home when I was eighteen, I have been able to receive funding for my personal care attendants through Medicaid and through Iowa Vocational Rehabilitation Services, whose professed goal is to help people with disabilities succeed in their career. Because attending college—both undergrad and graduate school—is needed for me to reach my IVRS goal of eventually teaching at a university, IVRS helps to fund a large portion of my personal care attendant hours, which is a relief, considering I only get six hours a day of care through Medicaid, and I need nearly around-the-clock assistance.

Once I become employed after graduating, however, IVRS will no longer fund my hours, despite the fact that having someone to help me use the bathroom, set up materials, and move to and from places is the most important job support I need. I have known this from the moment I moved to Iowa City to attend college, but I have always been able to push it away from the current reality in front of my eyes, until, of course, I can push it away no longer.

I facilitate a Zoom meeting with myself, my case manager through the Iowa Department of Human Services, and IVRS in the fall. We go over all of the above facts, measuring my situation from what seems like every angle. We do not come up with a solution. At the turn of the new year, I send a follow-up email to IVRS that turns into an exhaustingly long email chain. It feels as if we are repeating the same facts and figures that we went over in the fall, that no one is willing to face the reality that I have carefully outlined for them: without IVRS's support, I will be down to six hours of care per day, which I cannot survive on. All this just because I would like to have a job, even while recognizing that our worth should not be determined by what we can "do," what we can "contribute" to society. All this, just because even with a job—unless I become a rocket scientist for NASA, like an older man I know with my same disease—I will not be able to pay for my own hours of care, on top of all the other normal life expenses, like rent and food and payments on services.

Within all of this, within this horrendous deficit of care, I see friends in the same position as I am faced with choices which are not really choices: Severely restrict their liquid intake, or get a suprapubic catheter, which would allow them to use the bathroom without assistance (sometimes), but requires a surgical procedure requiring anesthesia which, along with the surgery in and of itself, has many risks for someone with a compromised respiratory system. Move in with their parents if their parents are still physically able to cover the hours of care not covered by government programs or move into an apartment with a roommate who will cover care in exchange for rent. Never mind the unlikelihood of the latter, or the ways such a relationship would be slippery to hold onto in a healthy form. Pay out of pocket for the hours of care needed if they can afford to do so, or end up moving into a facility, where they will have next to no freedom, next to no autonomy, and will not receive the care they need, due to the sheer fact that this branch of healthcare is understaffed and their workers are underpaid.

I try to explain all of this to my case manager and to IVRS, and when I feel myself sliding into hurt, frustration, and anger over this situation, I tell myself I am done defending my right to access the care I need in order to live, just for the day, or at the very least that afternoon. I step away from my computer, I break off a piece of chili-spiced chocolate that was a present from my brother and place it in my mouth, and I go over to my grandparents' house with my mom and my cat.

For a while, I feel lighter. On the way home from my grandparents, as my mom and I are driving down the road with a foot and a half of snow on either side of us, I say, "I think it's all going to work out. I think the IVRS thing is going to work out."

After dinner that night, I open my email—we're in the first week of the semester and I've been fielding an influx of questions from students—and see a long email from the IVRS supervisor. She understands it must be frustrating coming up against these barriers time and time again, and that my determination does not go unnoticed, and that I am a great self-advocate. They are, she says, excited to see what my future holds.

"Future" being something, of course, that they will not support me in. "Barriers" being only those which they had no part in creating. "Self-advocate" being what I must do to be given the care I need to live, "self-advocate" being communicating over and over again the facts of the situation and demanding I not end up in a nursing home, "self-advocate" being doing their job for them.

Thank you, I appreciate that, I write back. *But I really want to underscore that it should not be this hard for anyone needing personal attendant hours, nor should people with disabilities have to be self-advocates to this level to get the care they require to live. It doesn't make sense to me that IVRS would have the goal of helping people with disabilities become employed, and then the moment we do become employed, take away the supports we need to be employed. I believe strongly that this is antithetical to what I would hope would be everyone's goal for people with disabilities to be supported in their contributions to society. The fact is I shouldn't have to fight for this. If I was willing to not fight—which, to be clear, I am fortunate to have the natural supports in my life to have the energy to do so—what would then be the option? For my hours of care to go down to six a day and probably live with my parents for as long as they were able to take care of me? Then what?*

I tell them I will not be responding to emails tomorrow, to give myself a break from the emotional drain of this back and forth. Again, I step away from my computer, feeling like there are burning embers just beneath my skin, threatening to dissolve the layer between myself and the world around me, my body turning into a bubble of repressed emotions repressed no longer. I go down to the kitchen, where my parents are talking to my brother on the phone, except the embers have grown into a roaring fire and I cannot concentrate on what my brother is saying—I can only concentrate on what he is *not* saying, which is the fact that if the system has its way, his sister's autonomy will be slashed and she will end up moving in with her parents, until her parents are not able to take care of her anymore.

I go back to my room, sit and stare at the painting on my wall above my bed: "You are enough and you have enough time." It's a quote from Karamo Brown in an episode of *Queer Eye. To the systems which categorize who gets what care, I am not enough,* I can't stop myself from thinking. *And what if we don't have enough time? What then?*

My mom can read the emotions on my face even if I employ all the tricks I've learned to hide them—even smile, steady nod, eyes not ready to release their bubble of tears because I have looked away and I have focused on the sound of our house creaking to ground myself in my body and I have swallowed that salty seawater back down. And so, after my parents say goodbye to my brother, my mom comes into my room, guided by a shred of intuition that something is not right.

"How are you doing? Are you doing alright?" And this is all it takes to pull the tears back up, to let the fire burn through my skin: the body as volcano.

My voice rises and shakes as I recount each thread of the emails to my mom. My dad, who must have gone to the basement after talking to my brother, is coming back up the steps, wondering why I am yelling.

"I'm doing their job for them!" I cry. "And they just give me a pat on the back and say I'm a good self-advocate when I am literally just demanding I have what I need to stay alive!"

I had asked about life post-college, life post-Vocational Rehab in the Facebook group I'm a part of for adults with neuromuscular diseases, and have been horrified at the sheer frequency of the scenario now facing me. So many people I'd met at conferences for people with Spinal Muscular Atrophy—people I'd sat through "How to be a Teen on Wheels" workshops with—were now living with their parents because they did not have the care they needed. And I was simply expected to explain this to the people who were working for the systems that designed these structures, because it was simply *expecting too much* for them to know the realities created by these structures they worked under. Explaining my reality over and over left my skin burning yet numb, my eyes overflowing, my stomach in knots. Are our bodies a drain on the system, or is it the other way around?

When I was at the University of Iowa, the office of Student Disability Services would only help me (and other students) so much, before telling us we had to learn to self-advocate, as if that wasn't just a way for them to shift responsibility away from themselves (and, apparently, up the staircase that led to the front door of their office. No, I'm not kidding. If you couldn't do stairs you had to take an elevator through the dingy basement and enter through the back door). Three years after I graduated, students "self-advocated" enough to get the offices of Student Disability Services moved to a more accessible and welcoming location. Students should never have had to do this. I wonder if the university's definition of "self advocacy" included actions such as these.

After cry-raging to my parents about all of this, I finally stop, and let the tears fall more freely. My parents say all the right things, smoldering in their own rage, and as I lay back in my chair and let Mercury nuzzle up to me (he, too, can read my heart), I think again of how lucky and privileged I am to have parents that will go to bat for me over and over and over again. I am lucky and I am privileged in this because this isn't always the case, and isn't that, really, the tragedy of this situation?

Later, I will think of another quote from Naomi Ortiz: "Small interactions which reinforce the silencing of my body as 'no big deal' adds to the weight of that silence making it feel dense and heavy. My anger seems to be all that succeeds in propping it up, keeping the silence from squashing me into complete retreat." But in this moment, when the fire inside of me has burned through my skin and the saltwater of my tears has no power over the flames, I feel like I could destroy something; I have the urge to completely smash into pieces the system of glass around me—glass which allows me to see out, to see just over the edge of what society has deemed fit and acceptable for bodies like mine, while still closing me in.

When I was a freshman in high school and my friend Caroline was taken off life support, I sat for hours in front of my bedroom window, seething at a world that could and had let this happen, imagining, over and over, my fist crashing through the glass of my window in an outward manifestation of the hurricane of emotions swirling inside of me. Later I would read *Catcher in the Rye* and sink into the relief of Holden's echoing my desire, a desire that he is actually able to act on in response to his brother Allie's death. It is this scene of Holden putting his fist through the window of their garage that makes it impossible for me to despise him, despite his misogyny and homophobia.

Years and years and years later, I would be lying in bed with a girl I was desperately attracted to but bound never to be with, and repeat this same sentence about Holden Caulfield as we both looked up at the pages from *Catcher in the Rye* I had pinned to my wall: *It is the scene of him putting his fist through the window of their garage that makes it impossible for me to despise him.*

I had not felt as alive as I did while raging about the impossible narrowness of the system's future for me in my bedroom to an audience of my parents in a long, long time. But this level of aliveness—this level of being awake—was not one I could sustain for longer than thirty minutes, because it turned my insides into a roiling, flowing, cauldron of lava, one which burned away all the hazy comforts we cloak ourselves in to keep our heads down and get through the day, the week, the month, the year.

How nice it would be, I thought, for someone else to take this lava and act with it, someone whose life and future is not currently being debated by individuals at work in a system that is set up to bar disabled people from autonomy. I have been living at home with my parents for most of the past eleven months, and familial mental health aside, we all know that having me stay here indefinitely is unsustainable, that my parents' bodies will not be able to indefinitely take care of mine. And all of this after nearly a year of being a part of a community viewed as collective collateral.

The regulations of what state Vocational Rehabilitation agencies can provide are set at the federal level, unlike the number of hours I receive through Home and Community Based Services (a program under Medicaid to provide supports for people with disabilities to stay in their homes), which are set by the state. My case manager through the Department of Human Services is an actual miracle worker, and writes an Exception to Policy with the help of Disability Rights Iowa that gets Medicaid to approve more than six hours a day, but still not enough for me to live on my own. She also finds a service through my county that will fund some hours of care while I'm working, but they operate on a sliding scale, meaning that the minute I start making around $1600/month, I have to pay some of the services back. When I start making around $38,000/year, the county services pull out completely, expecting me to fully fund that service. To do so would leave me with no money, literally. Soon, I will be back to square one. My case manager will have to write more and more exceptions to policy, which will hopefully get approved for me to have more hours of care. There is no guarantee, though. We are fighting against the odds. And even if an Exception to Policy is approved to give me around-the-clock care, this doesn't account for the sheer lack of people willing to work caregiving jobs at such low wages, nor the other people in my same position. Instead of changing a broken system, we have to pour time and energy into finding workarounds.

There's a group of other disabled Iowans who I do advocacy work with, trying to dream up better realities, a more sustainable world. This group, and those who came before us, has done incredible work to address the inequities in care under Iowa's Medicaid. And we're still fighting. I'm still yearning for a web of care, a supportive and reciprocal and thriving ecosystem of love and community like Leah Lakshmi Piepzna-Samarasinha also envisions. This is in stark contrast to the way the current structure operates, but this ideal of *what it could and should be* is what keeps me involved in trying to make it better. Still, what isn't talked about enough: after you've spent so much energy simply fighting to stay alive, fighting to stay afloat, there's not always much left for trying to change the systems which pushed you under in the first place.

In the year after I graduated from the University of Iowa, while I was occupying that weird liminal space of someone who knew they would be leaving soon and thus their time in that environment was constantly dwindling, I met Haley for dinner one night at Pullman Diner. I had been badgering her for the past year about needing to be informed about politics and what was going on in the world and involved in making it better. I saw things in black and white then—it was how I learned to survive.

"I just think I was made to make my little corner of the world better," Haley said over delicately fried pickles and kombucha crossed with beer. "Meaning, I can change the world by my day-to-day interactions with people. I don't *know* enough about politics or what else is going on."

What I would tell Haley now, if I was back in that diner, eating our overpriced food and looking out through the glass at the Iowa City sidewalk: you are 100 percent right, you *can* change the world in your day-to-day interactions with people, but a part of that means fully understanding the extent of what is happening to the people you interact with and then going to bat for them when they need a hand.

Years later, I would come across this quote from South African cleric and anti-apartheid activist Desmond Tutu: "There comes a point where we need to stop just pulling people out of the river. We need to go upstream and find out why they're falling in." And I have yet to meet anyone as skilled at pulling people out of the river as Haley is. I doubt I ever will—when she sees someone being mistreated by someone else, she never looks away. When I feel my heart breaking over and over because I am forced to recognize that I can no longer stay beside someone I had built dreams with, she always says the right thing, never "You will find someone," but, "You are strong and you can get through this." When I have interactions with helpers that leave me feeling like I am wrong and selfish for wanting my needs to be met, she makes sure I understand that I am not, and that I deserve better. But in this moment in Pullman Diner, being pulled out of the river is not what I need, because the systems that be have continued and will continue to throw me back in.

"I know," I said, sharply aware of the tears stinging my eyes and the lump rising in the back of my throat. I loved Haley fiercely, and wanted to always believe in the shining friendship we had created and could create. "But that's not enough. We need the people who don't feel like they're directly impacted by politics to be invested in politics, or things are not going to change. I don't have the energy to always be fighting for what I need and what my community needs, because it is my life—and my humanity—on the line." Of course, what I was actually saying is one of the most elemental human phrases uttered throughout time: *I need help.*

V. THE BODY AS EXPERIMENT

The day that I take my first dose of Risdiplam is altogether extraordinarily common. It's the second FDA-approved treatment drug (not gene therapy, like Avexis) for my disease, and unlike Spinraza, this drug does not need to be injected into my spinal fluid. Risdiplam and Spinraza have, at the time of my first dose, not been tested against one another to gather data on differing rates of efficacy, and so, in some ways, I feel myself becoming an experiment, a body that will produce data over the next however many years, data which will be offhandedly gathered at appointments with neurologists, where I'll be asked to describe what my body can and cannot do and be expected to trust my own words. Risdiplam gets shipped to my address in a small, refrigerated box. It comes with its own syringes. It tastes like strawberry candy. There is no pomp and circumstance involved.

My first injection of Spinraza was painful and stressful and momentous. This, this act of my mom drawing up the 6.6 mL of clear liquid, of putting the end of the syringe into my mouth and pushing down the plunger, feels as if it only takes on meaning from the events swirling around us—the death of disabled people, the limbo of the pandemic, the threat of losing the hours of care I need. The decision to transition from Spinraza to Risdiplam is not hard, even as its dosing is daily instead of every four months. What's less easy, though, is my continual wrestling with ideas of luck versus privilege.

"Update, the Risdiplam tastes good," I text my friend and fellow Harry Styles fan, Brooklyn, that afternoon. "*Tastes like strawberries, on a summer evening,*" she responds. Brooklyn also has SMA. "Wait a second . . ." I shoot back. "Is Risdiplam . . . the box?" Later, I Tweet this. A Twitter account, Mary, with "CureSMA" as her banner and #curetype3too in her bio likes my Tweet and responds with "you have no idea how lucky you are!"

I am lucky, and here's why: despite the horrendous inequities in the United States's healthcare system, and despite the very specific way the US has conveyed disabled lives as disposable during this pandemic, I have access to Risdiplam, which, if not covered by insurance companies, is (generally) covered by the drug company. After scrolling through Mary's Twitter, I realize she lives in Cuba and has a link to a GoFundMe page for medical support, discussing how little support she gets from the Cuban government. Risdiplam is not approved in Cuba. In fact, at the time of my first dose, Risdiplam is not approved in most countries, including Canada, where Brooklyn lives. Am I lucky or privileged or both?

Another example: most of my disabled friends have not been able to be as selective with their helpers during the pandemic as I have been. Brooklyn, for example, can't go home to her parents because her dad works in a hospital. Numbers are less daunting in Canada than the United States, let alone Iowa, but still. When my helper quits because he's "disheartened" that I don't trust him to follow safety precautions, this is all I can think about—this guilt of being *able* to be home with parents who can take care of me, who can work from home, who are taking this as seriously as they should be.

If one of my disabled friends dies from this, I will never forgive you, I think over and over and over throughout the first few months of COVID-19, every time I see a friend or acquaintance post a photo of themselves with a group of people, huddled close and masks off. And now here we are. And though I haven't lost a close disabled friend to COVID, our community will always suffer losses, have suffered so many losses, now and before. I hope I'm not squelching a narrative out of this for narrative's sake, I hope I am not limiting no-longer-living, no-longer-breathing people to political currency, I hope I am not failing to allow for the contradictions living within us.

VI. THE BODY AS REMEMBERED / THE BODY AS WITNESS

Caroline got her eyebrow pierced for her seventeenth birthday, something I interpreted as a defiant act of reclaiming autonomy over her body, a body that had been nearly stripped of its autonomy in so many instances, by so many outside forces.

I was at her house the night her mom and aunt came to take her to the piercing place. Caroline lived in a group home, a ranch house with a long ramp up to a large back porch, an open living room and kitchen, and at least five bedrooms down the hall, all with each resident's disability-specific equipment, plus all the usual items and decorations that show a bedroom is lived in. Since teenagers and young adults lived here, that meant posters of the cast of Twilight, sports memorabilia, and photos from concerts.

At the time, I resented Caroline's family for Caroline's living situation. Caroline did not have an intellectual disability like the other young adults living there, and I saw her reality as one of someone who was trapped.

I want to be very conscious about resisting the disability hierarchy built into our society and am in no way suggesting that Caroline was *better than* her housemates because of the specificities of her condition versus theirs. What does feel true, though, is that Caroline had different needs than her housemates, and these seemed just out of reach. I don't know where I fall on the general argument of group homes for people with disabilities, now—the topic seems intrinsically woven with class and socioeconomic status, and how Home and Community Based Services under Medicaid are severely underfunded, and generally poorly run.

My hometown hosts the headquarters of ChildServe, an organization providing services for children and young adults with disabilities, and because of this, there are many group homes where I live, many children and young adults with disabilities who I went to school with. Although many of them were and are separated into different classrooms, I knew many of them well because I would go to one of their classrooms throughout the day to use the bathroom, as none of the "accessible" stalls in the hallway bathrooms were accessible to fit my specific needs.

One day in middle school, my helper and I noticed that one of this class's students had a really red eye. When we asked one of the associates about this, she said that they thought this was because his bi-pap mask wasn't on correctly throughout the night and was blowing in his eye. This meant, I assumed, that he probably hadn't gotten any sleep, that he spent around eight hours in physical discomfort because he was unable to communicate his needs to his caregivers in a way that they could understand.

I used a bi-pap machine at night as well, to help me take deeper breaths and thus sleep better. The fit of the mask is so specific that it can sometimes take close to ten minutes to get the position just right, so that there is no air leaking out onto my face. The type of mask I currently use has little "nasal pillows" which rest inside my nostrils, but for a long time when I was younger, I used a type of mask that sealed around my entire nose, with a strap that went up and across my forehead. To get this mask tight enough so no air would leak out the sides, we had to pull the cloth straps to such a degree that some mornings I would arrive at school with small bruises on my face. The intricacies of the bi-pap mask were a problem I knew well, but unlike the boy I went to school with whose eye revealed a sleepless night, I could verbalize to my caregivers how the mask needed to be positioned so that I could sleep.

This boy had lived at home with his family until his mom developed Parkinson's and could no longer give him the care that he needed to the level at which he needed it. When he was moved into a group home, my helper and the associates in his classroom spoke in hushed voices about how hard this was for his mom, how she felt like she was failing him, how there was nothing, they all agreed, she could do.

This was perhaps not a conversation I was meant to be a part of, information I was perhaps not meant to overhear, a perpetual position I found myself in from my earliest memories and even before—*because we carried you around for so long when you were little, before you got your first wheelchair, you were on the same level of adults, a part of adult conversation*, my mom would tell me, once. This was perhaps part of the reason why I started speaking so young, why there are home videos of me at sixteen months forming the names of those around me, proclaiming the activity I had imagined for myself, describing what I had done that day. And now here I am, years and years after I heard everything that was said that day about this boy's mom, about his move into a group home, thinking about how much we expect from parents and how little we ask of our culture, how the concept of *it takes a village* is splintered in this country, into empty words.

I don't know how old Caroline was when she first started talking verbally. I don't know if she was hoisted up and bounced around by her parents and held at face level of all the adults around her. It wouldn't surprise me if she also started talking really young, if she also overheard conversations not meant for her ears.

One year at camp, there was a new camper, Lily, who was talkative and bright and quick-witted far beyond her years. I sat next to her one morning while eating breakfast, barely a teenager myself, and was floored by the level of conversation I had with this seven year old.

"I'm sure she grew up fast," my counselor told me later, when I mentioned this to her. "Kind of like you."

I don't know why Lily had to grow up fast. She used a motorized wheelchair like I did and had ankle braces like I did, but Lily was also trached and so, I guess, had more intensive medical care than many of us at camp. Maybe she was also carried around as a toddler, a part of adult conversations. Maybe she simply had become so used to her body being cared for in ways starkly different from those around her that she had shed the coat of childhood early, had stepped into her role as adult because she had no other choice. How cruel, the ways many disabled individuals are both robbed of their childhoods yet not allowed to grow up, stuck in perpetual Neverland.

When Caroline's mom and aunt came to take Caroline to get her eyebrow pierced, I was at Caroline's house, the group home she lived in, visiting another friend who I knew through school. When her mom came in, I witnessed the harried energy, the *well, we need to get this done so I can get to the hotel*—at least this is how it stuck in my mind. This was part of what went into the definition of *trapped*, the definition of *this isn't fair*.

Nearly a year later, I would be at my grandparent's house goofing around with my cousin Sarah when my mom would come in through the front door, a look of *god I don't want to have to say this but here I am, the messenger* in her eyes, a look that made me stop. "It's Caroline, she's in the hospital." This was all she said, but somehow it was immediately clear to me that this was not just another hospital visit, something I had become used to in my own childhood. This was something that meant somewhere near the end, and I let my mom wrap her arms around me while I sobbed into her shirt, repeating the word *no* over and over.

We try to make her death mean something. *Her* being plural, *her* being subjective, *her* being, of course, so many people. I'm fourteen years old and there is no pandemic yet, but illness still kills, especially if your life keeps slipping through the cracks of what society has deemed valuable.

When I was younger, I clung to the details of Caroline's family being sprawled in the hospital wing's family room, appearing as if this was nothing big to them, their soft drinks and cell phones clutched in their hands. The hospital wing is familiar to me—at this point in my life, I had done many stints at Blank Children's Hospital in downtown Des Moines, and I knew the deep blue of the walls, the pretending-to-be-fun shapes on the carpet, the fish tanks in the family rooms. As I sat in the same room as her family, then, I know with certainty that my shoulders were hunched under my zip-up hooded sweatshirt, that my face held the set look I would carry with me through the rest of high school, my jawline hardened into an aggressive resolve.

The last time I saw Caroline, she was hooked up to machines. Her eyes looked out over the bi-pap mask on her nose. I want to be able to say her eyebrow piercing shone, that it rested on her eyebrow as a steady reminder of her personality and spirit. But I don't know if it did, really, or if an eyebrow piercing can act as an adequate symbol in this instance. There is a difference, I think, between the piercing itself as it existed in Caroline's body, versus the eyebrow piercing that I am invoking as a symbol in an essay trying to make sense of my friend's death.

In the room with Caroline was the mom of the boy she had gone to prom with. She was happy to see me, seemed chipper and bright. *What is wrong with you?* I thought, never realizing how witnessing death can make someone act in all sorts of bizarre ways, as they struggle to hold on to what they've known as reality. Until now, I never even realized that this mother was perhaps worried over how to relay all of this to her son, was perhaps *seeing* her son, who also had a disability, in Caroline at that moment. And yet: *Caroline is dying, what is wrong with you?* pounded at my temples.

Over the next year and a half, I collected different bits of information about my friend's death: Caroline's housemates had not been allowed to visit her in the hospital, and she'd told our mutual friend, who would be my helper in high school, that she wanted to live. She wanted her fingernails to be painted red, and so her mom, who my teenage self hated for leaving her in a group home, left the hospital to go get her daughter red nail polish. Her mom wasn't there when she died.

For a time, then, my life became separated into Before Caroline Died and After Caroline Died. I was a teenager battling anxiety and depression, hating my own skin, feeling like the definition of home would never include my body. But in the wake of Caroline's death, I clung to a seeming truth that I could make sense of: Caroline was bubbly and outgoing and unapologetically flirtatious with boys. She saw what she wanted and reached out to grab it, despite her desires continuing to evade her. How, then, did I expect my own desires to be fulfilled if I kept tiptoeing around them, refusing to let them fit into the shape of words? And what if the shapes of the words I knew weren't big enough—what then?

I let my anger and hurt spill over the edges of myself in cruel streaks. I took pieces of Caroline and created a Facebook profile of a girl named Turtle, who messaged Caroline's grieving mom to tell her that Caroline was at peace, and that she should be too. I believed I was doing the right thing, grasping at any story I could to make sense of this new, broken world I found myself in. I don't know, really, what I meant by my message—did I actually believe that Caroline had found some sort of peace in death? What did this mean for her as she lived?

It wasn't until I received a message from her mom's friend through Turtle's account, raging at my cruelty, calling me a bitch, that I even realized the way my words and actions, meant to be a release of some sort, were instead the cause of harm. I was a teenager reeling in a shattered reality, attempting to put back together shards of a world that let my friend die, that allowed bodies like mine to disappear. This is not an excuse for the way I shaped my hurt and how I directed my anger, only context. After the angry Facebook message from her mom's friend, I deleted the account, scrubbed any evidence of my connection to Turtle from the internet and my computer. Until, of course, now.

Years later, I tried to right this in a way I knew how—I wrote a message to Caroline's mom through the memorial website that had been set up for her. I can't remember the exact words I had written, but I know they held the hope of an apology, for her loss but also for any harm I had ever caused.

How quick I am to judge the mothers of disabled kids. Ten years has given me time to accept that grief manifests in different ways for different people, but ten years has not given me time to accept how easily some bodies are simply seen as bodies.

I went on a walk with Sarah the day after Caroline died, after I had sat in front of my window and pictured my fist made bloody by the breaking glass; the sun shone down on us and it was warm for March. I hadn't told her, yet, about Caroline's death. I didn't yet have the words to hold the weight of how my understanding of life had shattered, and the age difference between Sarah and I meant that I saw it as some part of my role as the older cousin to shield her as best I could from darkness.

We went on walks a lot together, as it was our way to get away from everyone else—the parents, or the grandparents, or the boys being boys. We could talk freely on such walks about our fears, about our wishes, about what we didn't quite understand about being girls in a world built for boys.

"I can give Caroline my kidney," Sarah suddenly said, her foot scuffing the sidewalk beneath her. "I mean, that would help, right?" Because Caroline's kidneys had been failing, had failed, past tense, time no longer halted, and here I was, faced with explaining to my eleven-year-old cousin and best friend that the world keeps turning.

I swallowed. The sunlight curved through my eyelashes. "Caroline passed away yesterday."

My journalism professor in college railed against euphemisms for death every chance he got. *Passed away, in a better place, passed on*. "And you know what I really hate?" he'd always say, the answer to his question something we could all predict because of how often he told us. "'They're with Jesus now.' What does that even mean? When someone dies, we write they died. We don't try to soften it."

Caroline died, and I softened it for Sarah, as I still have the tendency to do, because *passed away* includes *passed*, which feels more like a transition and less like an ending, and clearly Caroline didn't end because here she is, here she is, here she is.

A tree was planted at my high school to honor and memorialize Caroline, and for the life of me, I cannot remember if I was there for the planting or not. I assume I was, but so much of my time in high school—the time following Caroline's death—is either harshly etched in memory or a foggy blur.

My art teacher Mr. Weiss was responsible for taking care of Caroline's tree, as he seemed responsible for taking care of so many living things. We would mark her birthdays in special ways, by creating artwork to hang with ribbon from the branches of her tree, by writing *Happy birthday, Caroline* in letters full of curls in the March snow.

One year, on Caroline's birthday, I was in the pottery room connected to the art room—both of which continue to appear, in various iterations, in my dreams—writing something in a notebook about paper airplanes and trying to form a story out of the ways I could and could not form shapes out of clay with my weakened hands. Caroline dying had turned me into a witness, a heaviness I did not know how to carry and still live. If I made myself light enough, I figured, I could fly away on a paper airplane. I only believed this logic in the context of a story, but the scratches on my wrist from an X-Acto knife, scratches I told my helper came from my cat, told a different truth of what beliefs my body held.

Weiss was teaching a class in the other room as I sat next to the pottery wheel and experienced something I would later learn to call a panic attack. Tears clenched my throat as I shrunk further and further inside myself, until my hands on my lap no longer seemed living, the details of the world in front of me surreal. The boy I had a desperate crush on was in the class Weiss was teaching, and as soon as the students were given time to draw on their own, Weiss, my helper, and I were going to go outside to water Caroline's tree and decorate it. The proximity of everything—loss, creation, attraction—lay heavy in my mind, and I had not yet figured out how to separate one feeling from another.

During the fall after my graduation from the University of Iowa, Weiss died, and when I called to tell my parents, I said he'd passed away. I still have not cried over his death in waking life, although once, not long after he died, I had a dream that he was on the other side of a hilly street whose upward slope I was running (not metaphorically) against. He wore the loose, cottony-white button-up that so often marked his appearance, and a familiar, excited smile. "Hannah!" he called out to me, raising a hand in a wave. And there was only one thing that I could do in that moment, one path on which the story could unfold: I knelt down on the concrete—knees pressed against the sidewalk in a way they never have been before—and sobbed.

Caroline was just shy of her eighteenth birthday when she died—that is, when she was taken off of life support. She had told my helper in high school that she wanted to live. I don't know if, somewhere between the time of her telling our mutual friend this and her family making a different decision, she changed her mind. I hope she did. I hope she was fully at peace with her ending, and that her death does not need to take on other meanings, other definitions. I hope her mom leaving to get Caroline red nail polish is symbolic of her family respecting Caroline's wishes.

Eventually, a stone bench was placed by Caroline's tree as well. The high school has since been turned into a middle school, the new high school overtaking an open field which was home for so long to the perfect Iowa sunset, the geese, and the clouds.

DREAM

The Accomplice

You have a dream one night that you are sinking your teeth into the doctor's bicep and that the taste of blood makes fur sprout down your spine, fingernails sharpen to claws, two pointed ears push their way through your hair. The doctor ~~tells you how he plans to slice open the person turned patient turned body turned skin lying on the metal table~~ listens to the low purr in his ear, never telling him what to do, just knowing how to apply the right amount of pressure to make him realize that putting the knife through the skin is, in fact, a brilliant idea, an idea of his own creation. Was there a similar voice whispering into the ear of the person turned patient turned body turned skin lying on the table?

MERMAID INTERLUDE

The Fifth Mermaid

Yes, some of my human friends' husbands knew about the king's plan. By extension, some of my friends knew about the king's plan. And some of them did not know explicitly about the plan, but once it became apparent what was happening, they did nothing to shut it down. This broke me, and the breaking never quite stopped.

At the end of the third week of my self-induced isolation, my best friend called me to see how I was doing. I was in the bathtub—this was a technique we all had learned by now, dragging the bathtub out to the main part of our houses or apartments so we didn't have to stay secluded in the bathroom. There was some talk, even, of bathtubs being made with wheels.

"I'm doing alright," I said into the mouthpiece, holding the phone over the side of the tub and leaning my body out of the water to avoid getting the electronics wet. I was decidedly *not* alright, but trying to explain this to humans had brought about a certain type of fatigue that I no longer knew how to handle. "What about you? How are you and James?"

"Oh, we're fine. Um," I heard her swallow through the phone. "They've added leg testing to James's list of tasks at work now." This was, then, why she was calling. I was supposed to respond here, I could tell. Say something about how terrible this all was, the way the king's plan was evolving and hurting everyone involved. *Leg testing, ha. What a joke.*

Of course, I said none of these things. I stared out the window at the cheery hustle and bustle of people going by, doing their shopping, their dining, their visiting of each other. All of their legs worked just fine. Of course they did. If they didn't, they'd be in their bathtub, shut away from everything going on. “Well, what the fuck,” is what I did say to her then. “That’s . . .”

“I know. It’s terrible. The king’s plan is evolving and hurting everyone involved.”

I pulled my upper lip between my teeth and bit it. I swallowed. I took a deep breath. “So what’s James doing, then?” Why did I ask this? Because guessing wasn’t good enough. The upper half of my body, the half out of the water, was getting cold. I shouldn’t have been trying to draw out the conversation any longer, but there was a part of me that wasn’t satisfied with not knowing.

“Well, he doesn’t have a choice. We don’t have a choice. What is he supposed to do? Refuse to do it?”

What I was supposed to say: “Right, of course. There’s nothing he can do. There’s nothing you could do. You all have no choice in the matter.” But I didn’t say this. I didn’t say anything. I looked, again, at the sun slanting through the window onto the floor of my living room and wondered if my best friend and her husband saw my hiding as a choice, even though I would be carted off into exile if I was found.

I lay the phone on the floor, then. I didn’t hang up, just set it down. I sunk back into the water, sending a splash over the side of the bathtub and onto the floor. Later, I would check to see if the phone had been ruined.

The Woman Speaks

Sometimes, when someone asks you how you are, they do so in hopes that you will ask them in return. I know this move well, as I practiced it often when I was younger, terrified to tell the truth about how much my mind and heart hurt but still looking for some way to speak. Now, one night in January, after I've moved back home to Iowa, I notice it from my mom.

We've just finished dinner and my mom is still sitting at the table, her hands wrapped around a mug of tea. It's one of my mugs from Kansas, with mermaids and mermen (and mercats and merdogs) on it. My dad is in the bathroom. I'm leaning back in my chair, hearting the songs that have been playing throughout dinner to save them for later.

"How are you?" my mom asks, causing me to look up.

"I'm good!" I respond, honestly. "You?"

There is the tiniest of pauses before she says, "I'm good," but her words felt like they were hiding something else.

"Are you?" I asked. Her eyes are holding back from spilling over, another experience I know.

"I just—It's just . . . Why are people the way they are?" She is crying now. "They're just . . . so disappointing."

"I know," I say quietly, guessing where this is going.

On her drive back from picking up food for dinner, my mom had heard a story on NPR about a family in California with two children with rare disabilities which made them both very high risk for COVID. Their whole life had changed because of the pandemic—usually equipped with a large team of individuals trained to support the two boys' needs, the onset of COVID meant these supports were limited, or lacking altogether.

"I just—I just . . . I want to ask people who aren't getting vaccinated if they realize how this is all affecting other people," my mom says.

I am crying by now, too—slow, steady tears down my cheeks. I hate not knowing what to say to comfort my mom. Of course she is right, *vaccinated* also a stand in for *wearing masks* or simply *seeing others' lives as valuable.*

All I can think to do is ask her if she has read "You Are Not Entitled To Our Deaths: COVID, Abled Supremacy & Interdependence," the piece by disabled writer Mia Mingus I shared earlier, the beautifully burning manifesto on the worthiness of our lives.

> You are not entitled to our deaths. You are not entitled to the deaths of our loved ones in the name of capital, privilege and "normal." You are not entitled to our silence about our pain and suffering and the wet tar grief that envelops us. You are not entitled to our fear and terror at the worsening conditions and chaos of this pandemic, wondering if we will ever be able to safely leave our homes again.

I have yet to hear a more accurate description of my feelings surrounding the pandemic than *wet tar grief.*

My mom had read it. "I know, I can't let it get to me," she says, wiping her eyes.

I shake my head. "No, you have to let it get to you."

They are not entitled to our silence. You are not entitled to our silence.

My mom knows the danger of silence well. She, more than anyone I know, speaks the words which need to be spoken to the people who need to hear them. Whenever she tells me about a difficult conversation she had, my stomach turns to knots at the thought of these same words coming from my own mouth. I know that my fear of speaking in certain contexts is rooted in my fear of abandonment—that I still have a fear of losing people as a direct response to voicing my truths, for speaking my needs. I am always amazed at my mom's courage to speak, a courage I also see in Sarah, and in so many other people close to me. It is what pushes me to continue my relationship with words.

The helper who was abusive to me my freshman year of college emailed me one night, seven years after I had last heard from her. Like so many times in my life where the world seems to shift a bit more rapidly than its slow turn on the axis, I am sitting in front of my bedroom window, looking out at the trees in our yard and the street beyond.

When I open my email and see her name in my inbox, I at first think it's not real, then a different person by the same name. I open it, and denial is no longer an option.

Here's what you need to know: The year after I graduated college, I wrote a piece for Rooted in Rights. a well-known disability rights blog, as a part of their #MeToo series. I wrote about the experience with this helper, explaining that the #MeToo movement did not belong to me as I had not (yet) experienced a form of sexual violence, but that there are similarities in all types of abuse, and that consent reaches far beyond sexual encounters. Easily recognizable, horrific acts of violence do not exist in a vacuum, something I desperately wanted (and want) people to understand. I wrote:

> At the core of consent is respect for another person and respect of that person's ability and right to make their own choices about their bodies and their lives. Consent is a particularly loaded concept in the context of forced intimacy, when there are certain things that disabled people must consent to in order to stay alive. It is a particularly dangerous evil when someone knows this truth and takes advantage of it, pushing people with disabilities to endure toxic behavior because they rely on this person to take care of them.

My helper, the one I had written about, had read this piece, and it had stuck with her ever since.

Her email is one of the most mature apologies I have ever received. She told me she hoped her email did not bring me more harm, and that she was writing to validate everything I had written, that she had treated me and others terribly, and that she was truly, deeply sorry. She wrote that she was not apologizing to absolve herself or ask for forgiveness.

The experience of watching the lights in my dorm lobby curve into stars through my unshed tears stayed with me beyond that moment. It stayed with me beyond the writing of that article. It was lodged in my body and so of course it made its way into more of my writing. As I read her email and my body reacts by turning hot and then being overcome with chills, as I rock back and forth, tears spilling down my cheeks, one line in particular stands out to me: *I have read more of your work and know you reference that experience again. I don't know if you were talking about me, then, or a different helper.* As I read this, and even into the next day, I am struck, over and over, with the same thought: *of course it was you, but it was never just you.*

I like bruises because they are physical indicators of pain. This is not so much to say that I like pain—I don't, really, but that I like proof of an experience. An abuser punches you and leaves a mark: the physical signifier of violence blooms before your eyes, and even though you may waver on the meaning behind such a symbol, it is still there. All the violence from an abuser but no mark left: how much more difficult to remember the truth of a moment.

Throughout the course of the years which followed the burning of the bridge, there would be times when I would falter, second guess the way I experienced that year. Not because I thought I had remembered things wrong or interpreted the story incorrectly, but because I would feel snippets of that relationship in others. And the common presence of such seedlings of violence could either mean that emotional abuse and manipulation are an all-too-common experience in the context of helper/helpee relationships, or that what I had experienced wasn't what I thought it was.

It was what I thought it was. As the huge number of people who shared the piece I had written in 2018 and said, "Me, too" can attest, being manipulated and made to feel like a burden by someone who has been hired to care for you is more standard than we'd wish. The thing is, even though I've felt the beginnings of this from other helpers—because I've worked hard to recognize such and communicate boundaries and expectations from the beginning—I have, for the most part, been able to handle these instances and ask for accountability before anything escalates. But this doesn't mean it's easy, and it doesn't mean I'm responsible for those situations of emotional abuse. It just means that speaking up when something feels wrong often leads to change.

To be clear, I have made mistakes as an employer. To be just as clear, the power dynamic has shifted as I've gotten older and my helpers have, for the most part, remained college-aged. Still, no matter the age difference, at the end of the day, one person is in a position of relying on another individual to help them live their day as they want to. This individual has the power to withhold care, or worse—context that will never not matter.

There have been other situations with varying stakes.

Once, when I was told by a much older man who I volunteered with that my pink hair was "flat out sexy, sexual harassment charges be damned." I stepped back from that work for two weeks while I waited for the situation to be handled by the group's leaders. But as I abstained from group meetings and conversations while he continued to have that space to talk, I started to get that itch under my skin, the feeling of something not being right. *Why should I have to sacrifice participating?* I thought. *I have just as much right to be a part of the group as he does, and I'm not going to let him take that away from me.* So, I put myself back in. And the group leaders did what they could to address what he'd said. And he apologized to me. And the minute I brought up setting some new guidelines for the whole group about creating a safe and inclusive space, he said he was uncomfortable and left. His apology included the line "I have always had the utmost respect for you." I wanted to know, then, what his definition of *respect* was.

Once, when my neurologist's nurse said, "I don't know how they do it" in reference to adults with SMA in front of me, all I could think was *did she really just say that? I mean, really?* The neurologist was the same doctor who had diagnosed me, and who had told my parents it "wasn't worth it" to put me in physical therapy when they'd asked. I guess the *So Many Angels* message had gotten to her, too. When I emailed the nurse explaining why her comment had been so hurtful (I had burst into tears the moment she left the room), she responded with genuine understanding and an apology. She said she had meant her comment in regards to the systemic barriers people with neuromuscular diseases had to navigate in order to get the care they needed, but that she realized this was not clear when she spoke. She said she would be more conscientious of her words in the future. I'm glad I sent the email.

Once, when I told a publisher I would not be participating in any Zoom events if they were not going to provide closed captioning and an ASL interpreter. These events were specific to the disability community, not that that should matter. *We are everywhere*, I wanted to say. *Can't you see that? Or can you not see it because we've not been given access to the places you're looking?* I only had the courage to tell the publishers this because another disabled writer I looked up to, The Cyborg Jillian Weise, had once publicly turned down a speaking opportunity due to it not being accessible. Her speaking up gave me the guts to talk.

And once, when I was told by the man I thought I loved that he had once heard an interview of some famous person saying it was essential to always tell someone when you loved them. I took this as permission to speak, and you already know that he and I eventually combusted, and I spent the next year trying to figure out which of the things he had told me were true and what wasn't.

After I told him enough was enough, our mutual friend, the friend through which I had met him, worked up the courage to say the same thing. And then another woman. And then another. The fallout from me telling him hurt, but it allowed me to walk away (word choice intentional).

That man told me a lot of lies. But he also told me some truths, and that was one of them.

The spoken word disappears once spoken, unlike words put down on a page. This is only partly true, though, by which I mean it's a statement that takes a stab at truth and is precise as words can be, which is to say it is a design printed a few centimeters off target, the image warped slightly by paint. The truth of this statement is dependent upon written words being stronger and more lasting than memory, and of that I am simply not certain.

I once had lunch with Caroline at the Panera in town, accompanied by my mom and Caroline's helper. I remember a newspaper held up in front of a face, a suit and tie, the superintendent of our school district sitting at a nearby table. He greeted us by name, we greeted him back. He asked how we were doing, we answered him. And then Caroline asked the question that would stay with me forever and then some—

"When will the high school get a new elevator?"

I wouldn't have been in high school yet, and so had not encountered the elevator myself, but had heard less than flattering stories about its size and smell and reliability. Now I watched as the superintendent hemmed and hawed, repositioning himself in his chair, trying to make himself comfortable in a newly uncomfortable situation. Newly uncomfortable for him, that is. He gave us no satisfactory answer.

This is how I want Caroline to be remembered: In control of the situation, doling out carefully measured words, the fulcrum on which a hierarchy of power shifted. I witnessed the un-apologies (from her and from him), the way his perception of us shifted under her command. From pleasant "young ladies" to fully-fledged humans, complete with thoughts and feelings and discontent. *Aha*, I thought. *So much for boxing her in*. A moment in time. An interaction which changed, well, everything.

A few years later I'd enter the high school, still on the wings of Caroline's death, and join our newspaper staff, writing my very first opinion column about our archaic elevator. Do you know the meaning of the word archaic? Old-fashioned, out of date, sexual harassment charges be damned, the pink hair was flat out sexy.

Some things I discovered while doing research for my piece: The elevator at our high school was not up to code, but our school got away with this by saying it was "grandfathered" in, meaning that at the time that this part of the high school had been built, the elevator was up to code with the ADA, and since no renovations had been done to that part of the building since then, having the elevator be tiny and rickety was not *technically* illegal. A previous Spanish teacher had gotten stuck in the elevator, and since there was no call button, was stuck inside for fifteen minutes before someone figured out she was missing, that the elevator had broken down. The not-up-to-code elevator, though not strictly illegal, *was* pushing the limits of the law, especially since it could theoretically cause a student to not have equal access to education. And most infuriatingly, I discovered the relatively minor dip it would put in our district's budget.

The people in the school district, I discovered, fell somewhere on the scale of being directly affected by the elevator and caring deeply about it, to not even realizing it was an issue. The upsetting thing, however, was that clearly, a large chunk of people *did* see the problem with the elevator, they just didn't make this problem their priority. People had known about the Spanish teacher getting stuck, but still, nothing had been done. I was not the first student who needed to use the wheelchair that had come through the high school and had found the elevator appalling, and yet no one before had listened.

To get the cost of a new elevator, I talked to the Director of Buildings and Grounds, our conversation taped on the little red voice recorder I used pre-iPhone to record my interviews.

"So," I had said, after we had exchanged pleasantries and pretended like I wasn't sitting in his office in a spirit of interrogation. "What are some of the main reasons that the current elevator in the high school hasn't been replaced?"

"Oh, definitely the cost," he had replied. He was a stocky, friendly looking, older man with salt and pepper hair and glasses. He probably had no idea that I was about to talk him into a corner. And I almost—almost—felt bad for him.

"Sure." I nodded, feigning understanding. "And how much would that be, approximately?"

"About half a million dollars. Quite a substantial amount of money!"

I agreed this was, in fact, quite a bit of money. "And so, I also know that the district is planning on redoing our stadium. How much money is being set aside for that?

"Well, that project's set at about six million dollars."

I didn't say anything. I let my little red recorder absorb our pause. I looked at the man across from me, thinking, *Caroline, this one's for you.* "And so, what's the issue with the elevator again?"

When I would listen to the recording of our conversation later to type up my notes, I realized that I had been fidgeting with the part of the recorder that covered up its USB port, leaving an intermittent clicking noise wrapped up with our voices. I gave a class presentation in fifth grade where I clicked the slideshow pointer on and off throughout the whole speech, a nervous habit. But this wasn't nerves, this was the *tick tick tick* of carefully measured anger.

I went into the high school on a Saturday morning a few months later for an AP World History study session. The classroom for this was on the second floor. The elevator had an "Out of Service" sign on it. I went to the school board, reminding them of everything I had put into words in the newspaper—the history, the anecdotes, the law. Students with disabilities must be given equal access to educational opportunities as their non-disabled peers, as outlined in the Individuals with Disabilities Education Act. If the current elevator had not already breached this legal requirement (and I argued that it had), it would any day now, and I, for one, had absolutely no qualms about taking further action.

Within a year, our high school had a new elevator. The shiny new walls and light up buttons made me smile each time I passed by. I tell this story not to say, "Look what I did," but as proof of what a question asked and an answer not given (all over a lunch hour in Panera) can do. I tell this story as a testament to the shapes which can be redrawn from sharpened pens.

The email from my old helper shows that it's possible for people to change.

I can't move forward believing none of that helper's email was genuine, because I have to believe things, in general, can get better. If I don't, it feels like I'm throwing in the towel on the whole "change the world" thing, and that's not in my heart and not in my story. Plus, believing the world is only going to get worse (and that people can't learn) feels like admitting defeat to the culture that wants me to stay shut in with barely enough care covered to live. It feels like shutting up and keeping my head down. And despite having days where my depression wants to get the better of me, going quietly into defeat is not my end game.

But the email shows something else, something, I would argue, even more important. Giving voice to things which need to be given voice to allows for growth, by which I simply mean the opposite of stagnation. Speaking up and speaking out allows for new possibilities. There have been times I've spoken and said the wrong thing. It is of course never as easy as simply opening your mouth or hands and letting the words fall out. But each time I speak I learn, and I think (and I hope) that I become more intentional, more authentic, and clearer each time.

And yet—there are instances where you *have* spoken, and you've spoken again, and maybe even you've spoken again but changed your words or tone. And the listening isn't happening, and the message isn't being received.

I tweeted this quote from J. M. Barrie, once: "Shall we make a new rule of life from tonight: always try to be a little kinder than is necessary." The man I thought I loved liked my Tweet, and I'd eventually be left wondering at the meaning behind *a little kinder*. How much kindness is necessary, and how much should be added after that? But how often we forget, how often *I* forget, about kindness to ourselves. The extra dose of kindness comes as a balm when you leave what needs to be left and return to what needs to be returned to.

One day, nearly a year into the pandemic, I wrote a letter I never sent, a letter addressed to a composite friend, with all the hurt I didn't know what to do with.

Dear ______,

The other day I was listening to a podcast episode about trees, and the person being interviewed has a tree stump and the word *unless* tattooed on his arm, in reference to the Lorax quote: *Unless someone like you cares a whole awful lot, it's not going to get better. It's not.* And of course this is the truth, but it's more than that, because we can care and care and care until our hearts hurt but if we don't do anything about this nothing will change. So we must care and we must act. And I don't necessarily mean marching in the streets, although this must also happen. But I'm talking about having those hard conversations with the people in our lives, saying, *Hey, I care about this and I want to do what I can to make it better.* These conversations may not be comfortable or easy or fun. But if we simply continue to not talk about the hurt that is happening in our world because it does not directly affect us, we are turning our backs and simply perpetuating the problem. It is in these small moments of conversation that we start enacting change within our own relationships and communities.

I have a very distinct memory of a time right after the 2016 election when my aunt was over at our house, and we were all talking about how we were going to navigate relationships with Trump voters, which included other family members.

The week following the 2016 election, I awoke early each morning with lead in my stomach, a feeling that only grew heavier as the day wore on. I spent a lot of time crying. I left a class midway through because I felt a panic attack coming on, one which arrived full-blown in the hallway of our English Philosophy Building. There were individuals in my classes, in my friend group, in my family who understood and were feeling the same way. And then there were some who had not voted for Trump, but did not seem to understand or experience the horror myself and others were feeling—a visceral, bodily horror.

Because of this and because of my positionality as a queer disabled woman, I wanted nothing to do with Trump voters in the time after the election. I would not be able to engage in an authentic relationship with someone who had voted for him, and I had absolutely no desire to fake anything. As my nuclear family—my parents and my brother—and my aunt and I all sat in our living room discussing this, my brother said something that has stuck with me and that I now believe to be true: the best thing we can do as allies to marginalized individuals and communities is to *not* cut those people out of our lives, but to have tough conversations with them. Because we were going to need those individuals to help create change in the future (which we did, in the 2020 election), and if we are in a place of privilege to have those conversations, then we must do our best—and I mean really do our best—to do so, because it is not the responsibility of those who felt most threatened—marginalized individuals—to bridge the gap.

I struggle sometimes with wondering if we expect too much from people, to make sure they're informed, to use their voice for good, to do what they can to make this world a better place. But if I start to expect less from people, surely I am shortchanging what I have to believe is inherent in humanity—the desire to leave the world a better place.

A year later, I will add two more paragraphs.

Here's another truth: long COVID is now classified as a disability under the Americans with Disabilities Act. My friend's daughter has MRIs taken to see why she is still fatigued and in pain, a year and a half after she had a semi-mild case. When the results come back, the doctors are baffled in their unknowing. She has a special team of medical specialists devoted to understanding how long COVID is affecting her, but this is all new territory, like bouts of nausea and extreme exhaustion. Do you see it now?

Here's one more: this isn't the first pandemic our world has seen. It won't be the last. Even if future variants of the coronavirus become less severe, that future does not erase the horror of the past, the pain of the present. If I end up being one of the "everyone" who gets COVID or a future deadly virus, I may have very mild symptoms, or I may not. I may end up in the hospital, or I may not. But my level of comfort in risking that should be my choice, just as it should be the choice of any of us with underlying conditions that would exacerbate the virus and more likely

> lead to intense hospitalization or death. And I can't isolate, just as so many of us with disabilities who rely on others for care cannot isolate. What then?

Twenty-one years after my spinal fusion surgery, I'm back in Iowa City for a doctor's appointment. Over breakfast in our hotel lobby, my mom and I discuss my mental health history, which, of course, can't be disentangled from my history of eating.

Swallowing a bite of blueberry oatmeal, I tell my mom that up until sixth grade, I'd been "pretty good." There'd been some anxious times in fourth grade, yes, and I ended up in and out of the hospital from various sicknesses, it was true. But compared to the darkness that hit me in sixth grade, years before then had been good. Although, I *was* very skinny, definitely underweight, which certainly contributed to my frequent illness. Why had I been so skinny?

"Hannah, you weren't eating," my mom said, gently.

"Oh." Maybe, after all, I remembered some of this. "Do you think that was due to anxiety?"

My mom swallowed, and the truth of that moment is that her eyes shone with the morning sunlight piercing through the windows.

And she told me, then: In the time after my surgery, my mom had been reading, somewhere, about combat veterans developing PTSD. Despite surgery and war being in many ways different (although what is surgery if not a war on your body?), my mom had stopped what she was reading, turned to my dad, and said, "I think Hannah has PTSD."

This admission sends a golden streak of clarity through my mind. It also breaks my heart. This was no longer just something I'd stumbled across while putting together grad school applications: the rate of PTSD in people who've undergone spinal fusion surgery is disproportionately high and, so, perhaps, all of these experiences and emotions I'd been trying to make sense of now had a name. Child-me had been visibly traumatized, visibly distraught, to the point that my mom found the same language herself, in research not even related to surgery. It's validating to know that others had also named my experiences, but knowing how frightened and alone I must have felt post-surgery makes me abundantly, horribly sad.

Eight-year-old me had been through so much. She had been through so much that she was still making herself known in the present. In moments of people leaving, in endings of all kinds, she shows up and tries to speak. She fractured in her present (my past), and the only way to make her whole again is to see her, listen to her, comfort her. To realize she is a part—an important part, but just one part—of me.

Eight-year-old me is trying to speak. I'm doing my best to listen.

There are ways in which my dad's mom comes back to him, the same as she was when she left him at nine. Sometimes, he is driving to work in the mornings and will look over at a car driving next to him, and for a split second will see Maizie in the back seat, her face turned to look out the window, a look of peace in her eyes. She is silent, but this, surely, is also her speaking. My dad tells me he loves when this happens, that he can move through the rest of his day knowing she was there.

She comes to him, also, through a painting I did my first year away at college, a painting which now sits on a shelf above my bed in the bedroom I grew up in. The painting is a multi-colored side profile of a woman's face, the top of her head morphing into fiery swirls. She looks down, something between a smile and a frown on her lips.

"Did you mean to paint two faces?" my dad asks me one night, pointing out the shape of another woman on the canvas. I hadn't.

"It looks just like my mom," he says, nodding.

It takes me a while to see it, and even then I'm not sure if I am seeing the same face born out of paint daubs as he is. But if you look at it long enough, there *is* another face, looking over the shoulder of the woman I had painted. Her mouth is parted slightly, as if she is about to say something into the ear of the other woman.

As much as I like to think of how I can ensure the world to be a better place when I leave it for those who come after me, my metaphorical daughters, I can't accept that time and thus stories are linear, are not, in actuality, more cyclical, more like the spiral I tattooed with a stick and poke on the top of my mom's wrist at the beginning of quarantine.

And when I start to visualize the future like this, I can look at my mom after dinner one night in the deep dead of winter, when the long days of darkness are clutched around us, and want to leave the world better for her.

I keep coming back to the image of my mom, my uncle, and my grandparents at the top of Lookout Point at Sequoia Kings National Park, my grandma looking around and saying, *Well, this is* not *going to work,* and everyone traipsing back down the side of the mountain again. I am thinking that maybe I've gotten it wrong, when I've imagined what my inheritance holds.

My great grandma, this grandma's mom, once got tired of waiting for her husband to knock down a wall in their house that she wanted knocked down, and one day when my great grandpa was gone, she got out the sledgehammer or crowbar (my grandma can't remember) and did it herself. What a way to speak.

"Did Grandma ever knock down any walls?" I ask my mom one night, trying to find a story of my grandma doing something just as badass.

"Oh no," my mom responded, "but I'm sure she wanted to. Grandma's not as fiery as her mom was." Maybe, or maybe her fire burns a bit differently. Maybe it's the way she no longer cooks huge meals for family gatherings, realizing the exhaustion at the end of the day isn't worth it. Maybe it's the way she washes her hands of arguments she no longer wants to be a part of. Maybe it's the way she said, *This will never work for our family,* and lead her husband and kids down to the base of the mountain, to a different home.

My grandma will tell me, after reading a book I recommended, that she was disappointed when the narrator talked of being dead.

I don't remember what you mean about talking of being dead, I texted back.

When she was in the coma after the accident, in her subconscious state, she believed that she was dead, my grandma said to trip my memory. *It was beautiful, but I always have a problem with that concept.*

My grandma doesn't like when stories end in the narrator's death. She agreed with me that the true ending of this book, where the narrator is surrounded by the women in her family and community, taking part in a ceremony and claiming her identity, is stunning. From certain angles, this is a small thing. There's no sledgehammer or crowbar, no wall torn down in a statement. But my grandma knows about stories, and she knows about endings. She knows what a character deserves.

It is high summer, and I am outside on the back deck of our house. Plant fibers have created the shape of a woman, a heralding horn raised to her mouth with one hand, her other arm behind her. She is drawn in white against the black pole of the umbrella, the same umbrella the spider had built her web on years and years ago. I had been looking for guidance on whether or not to put words to a particular hurt, and here it was, plain as plant silk—*Speak,* the woman told me. *They are not entitled to your silence.*

They never are.

In a dream I push through the earth's topsoil like the newly sprouted growth in the meadow, and as I open my mouth to cry out, flowers burst forth.

The Water Essay

The sky through the window was a vibrant shade of purple, the color of sunsets, except this was not relegated to the place where the earth met the sky. It was the same shade I imagined heaven would be. I am thirteen, the year before Caroline will die, and am sitting in a hot tub at our hotel in New Mexico, surrounded by walls made of that orangey-brown mud that everything in New Mexico seems to be made of. We were there to pick my brother up from his summer job, and I fell in love with the land, how it felt in direct, beautiful contrast to Iowa's trees and fields and meadows.

I thought the purple sky was the best thing about New Mexico, so great that I thought this would make a great first line to a story: *The sky that day was purple.* It was delightfully upending. Still, my memory of the purple sky is inextricably connected to a feeling of sharp pressure around my chest as I sat in the hot tub. When submerged underwater, my lungs struggled to pull oxygen in, the weight of water immeasurably more than air. This was the first time I consciously understood what this heavy feeling in my chest meant, and all my interactions with bodies of water in the future would be shaped by this knowledge.

When I did water physical therapy throughout high school and part of college, I learned exactly when the chair attached to the side of the pool which was lowering me into the water needed to stop in order for my lungs to still work. "Too low," I would sometimes say to my physical therapist if her thumb had stayed too long on the button, and I would rise again. But in this heated water pool, as in the pool at the summer camp I would attend with Caroline, I could lay on my back supported by a foam noodle under my head and—somewhere in between the level of movement I have on land and the level of movement I have in my dreams—move around.

Water allows me to move my limbs freely, facilitating my obsession with mermaids as beings who simply need the right environment in order to thrive ("the disabled mermaid is only disabled on land," I would write as a line to a poem). Water also could kill me. The freedom that water affords me exists in a very narrow chasm—keep too much of my body above water and I cannot move, let myself sink too far, and my lungs are crushed.

I bring my cat home from the vet after his dental exam—an exam that included three tooth extractions—and wondered immediately if I had only done him harm. My mom opened his carrier in my bedroom, and we had to coax him out, a blue bandage wrapped around his front leg where they had given him an IV. The vet has told us it takes forty-eight hours for anesthesia to wear off entirely after a procedure like this, and in that moment, he stumbled from his padded carrier to our hardwood floors, making my stomach lurch.

"It might be hard to see him like this," my mom had said in the car, but Mercury was in his carrier strapped into the front seat of the van, and as I was sitting directly behind him, strapped into my wheelchair which was strapped into the van, I couldn't see what "like this" meant. From what the vet had said, however, I assumed that Mercury would be out of it and "wobbly," a word the vet tech who had brought him out to our van in a mask said while placing him on the front seat, a word repeated multiple times in the take-home care instructions I paged through that night.

Once we offered Mercury water (which he stared at but did not drink) and made sure he was settled (although he did not look comfortable, crouched as he was, not curled into his usual cinnamon roll shape), my mom helped me use the bathroom by lifting me onto my shower chair and wheeling it over the toilet. As I sat there and she left to check on Mercury, I started to cry ugly panicked tears, the thought *ohmygod I've done the wrong thing I've failed him* sputtering around and around and around in my mind.

"I know it's the hardest thing, seeing something you care for hurt," my mom said, when she came back in to help me and saw me crying. And while it might feel a bit of a particularly lesbian writer stretch to compare Mercury to my child—to say I was suddenly bent over in agony at the thought that I had harmed what I had chosen, four years ago, to take care of—my mom's words caused my mind to flash to an eight-year-old me sobbing hysterically while being wheeled back to an operating room, an eight-year-old me telling my mom everything would not be alright, an eight-year-old me waking up in the ICU and begging for ice chips to be put to my lips, where I can then lap up the melting water. *It was the hardest thing we ever did, but we had no choice.*

Mercury is FIV-positive, which is like being HIV-positive for felines. He also has gingivitis, which, if not for also being FIV-positive, would not be a big deal. But, because his immune system is not up to par, the usual inflammation of gums can turn to infections which can then turn to more serious problems, like needing to have infected teeth removed.

That evening, my mom will hold Mercury while she reads on the couch, and I will watch, helpless, as my parents give him the pain medicine and antibiotics he's been prescribed. He will hate this and fight them, and we all try to figure out the best way to do this, as he is not supposed to jump to or from heights in these next forty-eight hours, while he still has anesthesia in his body.

Before I even think about where Mercury will sleep that night, as he usually curls up next to someone, often going from one person to the next, my mom says something that shows she has clearly already figured out what to do.

"I'll sleep with him on the floor, I don't mind." And she didn't mind, she would assure me. She liked sleeping on hard surfaces (this was true).

The next morning, when my mom would get me up and I would immediately ask how Mercury was doing and thank her, again, for sleeping on the floor beside him, she would say, "Well, of course—it was the right thing to do."

And then, also—the way we play Brandi Carlile's "The Mother" over and over and over, belting out the narrator's affirmation that her daughter was no accident, and like her parents, she would grow to fight the power.

Power, as in: the doctors who told my parents it wouldn't be "worth it" to put me in physical therapy as a child. Power, as in: the stories that say disabled and sick people are too much of a distraction, are better off dead. Power, as in: the systems that make it damn near impossible to live.

There was the time when I had blood (90 percent water) drawn and the lab technician placed my arm right in front of my face instead of off to the side. I could have averted my eyes or closed them, but I didn't. A part of myself, a deep red, sticky part of myself, was being siphoned out of me through a needle in my vein. I felt woozy and lightheaded, a feeling akin to what my mom would feel every time I had to have blood drawn or IVs put in during my childhood hospital days, and she would have to put her head on the counter in the ER while I screamed and cried tears (98 percent water) in defiance of being poked and prodded against my will.

Once upon a time, a man I thought I loved told me that he didn't view disability as an anomaly, anymore. He said that all humans have their trials and barriers. Abnormal and anomaly are very similar words. I'm sure this made him uncomfortable. The man I thought I loved knew Nuala Ni Dhomhnaill's mermaid, my dear "Mermaid in the Hospital," the fictional character I loved so much, and because I was so entranced by his words, I took this as a sign.

Years and years after my spinal fusion surgery, and a year after disentangling myself from the man I thought I loved, my nightmares of being cut open on a surgical table are replaced by something altogether different: I am in an examination room, partially clothed, and the doctor is trying to show me images of my spine. *You have to look at them, Hannah,* he keeps telling me. *You have to see.*

I was in Ireland the first time I learned about the term *abject*—that which disturbs order or identity. Bulgarian-French philosopher and feminist Julia Kristeva argues that the *abject* is whatever is rejected by social reason. The abject happens, Kristeva says, when one is confronted with something that they wish to keep separate from themselves, or their sense of self. This seeing yet not seeing, this sawing off of a part of oneself, leaves people with a feeling of horror. In Ireland, the teacher of our Irish novel class explained *abject* by saying that it was often used to describe menstrual blood. A section from Nuala Ní Dhomhnaill's poem, "The Assimilated Merfolk"—

> The air of the tune is forever breaking down
> along with the menstrual rags, the menstrual blood
> they shy away from, reminiscent as it is
> of the ooze and muck
> from which it sprang.

I started taking birth control when I was in sixth grade, the same year I got my period. The concept frightened me, at first, maybe because I didn't know how to wrap my mind around the possibility of altering or controlling what my body was doing, as someone with an already fraught relationship with my skin and its contents. But I would bleed through my pants on almost a daily basis, so I finally gave in to my mom's pleas and started swallowing a tiny green pill every morning. I stopped taking them the January of my senior year of college, because at this point, I wasn't sexually active and would go through periods of wondering why I was taking certain medications.

After I stop taking my birth control, I don't have my period for about six months. And then it comes back with a vengeance, the kind of attack that makes one of my helpers scream every time he has to help me in the bathroom and makes me want to curl into a ball the first day and the few days prior to it every month. But then my friend gets pregnant. She's a year younger than me and her boyfriend's condom broke. And suddenly, whenever I find myself wishing I could crawl into the corner and die, I remind myself that I could have a tiny ball of life growing inside of me, possibly giving my body more purpose, possibly destroying it.

Risdiplam, the medication I transition to off of Spinraza, the treatment drug for SMA that can be taken orally daily and tastes like strawberry candy, will also harm any children I decide to have in utero. While having a Zoom appointment with my neurologist to begin the transition process, she goes over these risks with me and asks if I'm willing to go on birth control while taking this drug. *Well, I guess I should ask you first, are you sexually active?* she says, and because I think well on my feet, I quip back, *Not during a pandemic.*

I'm not willing to go on birth control, given the fact that I don't see my near future to be one in which I have sex with someone who can make me pregnant, and I'm also not willing to come out to her. I haven't even officially come out to my grandparents, although by now I assume—perhaps wrongly—that they already know. So eventually I just tell my neurologist, *Look, I'm not hooking up with guys*, and she says, *Ok, so you're not having casual sex?* And I say, *Sure.*

My wish to not give birth stems from reasons that could be perceived as selfish, although perhaps are simply modes of self-preservation: I know that nine months of carrying another life would sap a lot of my own strength and significantly drain my body of its already dwindling abilities. But I know that it's possible; other women with SMA have given birth and raised children. And I know that what physical assistances I could not perform for my child, such as changing a diaper, a helper or partner could perform for me, despite many people's belief that disabled individuals cannot parent, that needing help is a mark of failure, as if it does not take a village, anyway.

If I ever decide to have kids, which I don't foresee in my future, but of course futures change, I know raising my child would be an adventure I would love and take seriously. If I ever decide to have kids, I want to be like Carrie Ann Lucas, a renowned disability rights activist and lawyer who founded Disabled Parents Rights, a legal organization fighting discrimination against disabled parents. Carrie Ann Lucas raised four adopted children before her death at forty-seven, each of whom had disabilities themselves. After her death in 2019, the *New York Times* published a piece detailing her life and work. The photo included in the article shows Lucas on a bridge, with her four children around her—two of which are also in motorized wheelchairs. It's a beautiful photo, and a beautiful testament to disability family and community. If I ever decide to have kids, this, I realize, is what I want. I want to adopt children who can see themselves in me, not go through the pain of childbirth. Ultimately, though, perhaps my desire to not give birth comes back to the deep-rooted need for me to be in control of my body, and the tendency to shy away from sharing it with anyone else, except in moments of heady surrender.

This is different from another, perhaps more talked about reason to not give birth as a disabled woman whose disease is genetic: that in choosing to get pregnant, in choosing to foster a new life, we are risking passing on the gene that carries SMA, a choice some view as inherently selfish, selfish in a much different way than my desire to preserve my own body's limited muscle function.

I will interview a friend and fellow SMA-er for a journalism project in undergrad, and she will tell me that she doesn't want to have kids, and that while she doesn't want to judge other people with SMA who do choose to have kids, she feels it is a bit selfish to pass on the gene. My friend's answer shocks me, and then makes me worry about what we've internalized and how that's informed the way we see each other. Her choice is her choice, for which I do not wish to discredit her, considering how often choice is robbed from disabled individuals. She has her high school senior photos taken out of her wheelchair, a choice she admits to making because she wants to distance herself from being seen as disabled.

I title the story I turn in for class "Getting Away From 'The Pool,'" *the pool* referring not to a body of water, but to how disability is seen by our culture, and in it, I discuss the ways my friend and I have handled our disability differently, but how our actions are perhaps fueled by the same desire to erase not our disability, but the separateness we feel forced upon us. The answer to separateness isn't more separateness, I know, and so I write that *the solution isn't making myself as separate from the pool as possible, it's doing everything I can to change society's perception of people with disabilities so I'm not scared to be associated with "the pool" in the first place.*

The disabled, as a group, have often been discussed in relation to abjection, in that our bodies, in all of their beautifully twisted disfigurement, remind able-bodied people of the imminent looming of their own aging process, a process which makes their body decline in function until it stops functioning at all. We are, one could say, a constant reminder of the true lack of control we all have over our bodies, even a constant reminder of death, the exact opposite of what was quietly growing inside my friend's body, the possibility of which leaves my body on a monthly basis in a river of red.

When we see mermaids, we do not see a reflection of who we will be at a later stage in our life; we see something altogether different. We see something that disrupts and disturbs, whether the mermaid in question has the head and torso of a beautiful woman or of a ferocious, fanged monster. And maybe this disruption comes more from the sight of something we recognize in ourselves than something we don't.

Do mermaids bleed in the way that humans bleed? How much of the oceans, the rivers they live in is their blood, their tears? Do mermaids feel pleasure, fuck, procreate in the way that humans do? Their tails surely prohibit this, surely make them something between human and not, an anomaly. Perhaps the space they occupy, as beings in between, is due to the fact that they spend their whole lives living in something that can kill us but also gives us life, perhaps because the image they see of our world comes to them filtered through the ocean and thus arrives warped and distorted. But does that mean it's wrong?

In the months after I returned from Ireland, I could not get Nuala Ni Dhomhnaill's mermaid out of my mind. At one point, I told Fi over FaceTime that mermaids in wheelchairs were like, a thing, to which he replied, "Oh yes, they're very much an archetype." The mermaid in the wheelchair is nothing new, as anger and hurt and splintering of the self are not original responses to trauma—responses, say, to being placed in the lap of a man you are terrified of. Responses, say, to friends unjustly dying. Responses, say, to an abandonment that could have gone no other way.

Your body will go through motions in a time of crisis. Motions that are completely detached from your mind. Sometimes, when you are younger, these motions will be self-harming—they will include X-Acto knives, and scissors, and pins that your father gave you for Christmas. But because you're not strong enough, these motions will never draw blood. You'll just be left with angry scratches that you later claim came from your cat.

Sometimes, these motions are harshly protective, proving that your body has a hard time making up its mind about what it wants to happen to it. It will nod when people ask you if you're okay, it will force food into your mouth and it will force you to swallow even though the food tastes like cardboard because otherwise you would starve. It will allow you to cry, and it will not let you stop until you finally feel able to continue living.

The man you thought you loved would later tell you that this makes sense. That while most self-harmers do so in order to see a physical manifestation of their inner pain, or because everything has gone numb and they want to feel something, your forays into physically hurting yourself stemmed from the fact that you had been hurt before, an incredible bodily trauma that had been done to you without your consent, but that you would not be alive without enduring. It was, this man told you, a way of taking back that power.

You think he was right, but then there is also the fact that you would get upset with yourself when you couldn't leave a scar, and the fact that the line of raised skin going down your back, the visible proof of your surgery, is a part of yourself you covet like a rare pearl.

I spend a lot of time thinking about rivers: the River Liffey which flows through Dublin to the sea, the Raccoon River my dad and his siblings chose as a stage on which to play God, and the Iowa River which cuts

Iowa City in half, which I never figured out how to use to quench my longing.

Another Irish poet, Eavan Boland, memorializes her own mother in her poem "And Soul," turning her into the water that Dublin is made of, remembering that "the body is, or is / said to be, almost all / water," water which never fails to find its way into words and languages: "*coast canal ocean river stream* and now / *mother*."

We know more about the surface of Mars or the moon than about our own oceans, 70 percent of the earth's surface. Our bodies are approximately 60 percent water, 7 percent blood, even if it's blood we acquire from someone else after surgery. How much do we not know about the body? If knowledge is equated to power and power is equated to control, how likely is it that bodily autonomy is simply a lie we tell ourselves to make us feel better?

When I was in Ireland, I told the director of the creative writing program that I wanted to be able to write about something other than disability. "Why?" he'd asked, to which I didn't have an answer, except that I refused to be pigeonholed into the narrow definitions of what I believed I would be allowed to write about.

"The word 'disable' doesn't just refer to disability," he said. "What do you do to bombs if you don't want them to go off? You disable them." I didn't know how I felt about this at the time, the term "disable" being used to refer to something not doing what it was built to do, but it made me think of the play we saw in Dublin, about two boys who manufacture bombs for the Irish Republic Army. The play ended with a sudden, blinding glare of light and a sound that shook the theatre. The two boys were unable to disable the bomb in time.

The idea that water can always put out fire is a fallacy. There have been far more nuclear explosions underground than aboveground, because the oceans seem to be a favorite testing spot. But the effects of these bombs are not quelled by the water. The fallout and damage is not even less than if they were to be tested on land, one could argue. It's just different.

I'm in a writing class, less than a year after coming back from Ireland, when I realize I'm not straight. Being in close proximity to an impulsive person can stir a sensation beneath the surface of your skin that straddles the line between panic and lust. Because I am intoxicated by the idea of giving up control, I ignored labeling this feeling for a while. Eventually, though, I must face it, among the company of those I feel I have at my command: words.

"I began to write in an Ireland where the word 'woman' and the word 'poet' seemed to be in some sort of magnetic opposition to each other," Eavan Boland told the poetry journal *A Smartish Place*. "I wanted to put the life I lived into the poem I wrote. And the life I lived was a woman's life." *And the life I lived was a disabled life.*

It can be a very dangerous thing to attempt to categorize an experience that defies being pinned down. My interactions with this girl left me feeling trod upon, bruised, but in an ever-delightful way. And that's the thing about that tight feeling in the pit of your stomach and the fuzzy feeling behind your eyes—you're relying on your mind to come in and decide what it means.

The merfolk's language doesn't have boundaries, and we're not talking about the boundaries needed in healthy relationships, such as letting people exist as people, or *I consent to this, but not this.* We're talking about the lack of boundaries on a piece of paper that makes paint bleed into water, that asks for a cracking open of what a word can hold, a push of shoreline into the ocean: "We can recognize at once, without any difficulty, / that everything in the language runs into everything else, / that there are no strict boundaries between one thing and another." The moon doesn't appear over the river, "up over the upstreaming it mooned." Things are turned upside down and inside out in the world of the mermaids. Things are turned on their head.

The mermaid in "Teoranna/Boundaries," the same mermaid in many of Nuala Ni Dhomhnaill's poems, doesn't understand how one thing can end and another begin, because that is how the merfolk's language functions. "We all ran into each other, you'd swear to listen to her, / like the different colours in an oily puddle / after a shower of rain."

In Kansas, a year into the pandemic, winter storms and record low temperatures cause my friend's apartment to flood after his pipes freeze and burst. At the same time, Texas experiences snow and ice and cold that they are not prepared to deal with, that they have, in fact, never dealt with before. Broken infrastructure, climate change, corrupt politicians: these are disasters brought about by our own hands.

My friend will send me videos of the inches of water covering his floor, his feet sloshing over the ruined carpet, his belongings in trash bags. He had knee surgery two weeks before, and is still in the process of recovering, still unable to fully bear weight on his leg, when his apartment is flooded. In the videos he sends me, I will see crutches leaning up against door frames, the adaptive equipment he has bought to make his apartment temporarily more accessible for him scattered throughout the rapidly changing environment.

Post surgery, my friend is grieving the loss of autonomy. *I'm struggling with feeling like I can't rely on my body*, he texts me, precluded by a message asking me if he can ask me something that he hopes is not hurtful. *Do you ever feel this way?*

This is, I tell him, something I struggle with a lot, something I have had varying relationships with throughout the course of my life, and mourning loss of function is normal and common and allowed. *I try to focus still on things I can do*, I tell him, *and find joy in those, while still allowing space to mourn*. This is something, I think, that too easily gets erased in counter narratives of disability—the need to acknowledge that losing abilities is hard. Hard because we have been taught we need these abilities, yes, but also hard because we want to be able to trust our bodies, bodies that we have come to love in our own fierce and haphazard ways.

My grandma will wake up one day to greet not just the morning but also a new pain in her shoulder, a pain my mom fears signifies a break, which in turn signifies bones so brittle they will snap at the slightest amount of *too much*. My mom will echo my friend's feelings, telling me she thinks my grandma is having a hard time with realizing that she can't trust her body in the same way she used to be able to.

There is, of course, no more of a link between water and mothers than the fact that life begins in water, in the primordial ooze that we crawled out of, the site of our shed tails and discarded scales, and in the water of our body which shifts and breaks and melds into not just a new state of matter but also a new being.

Caring for someone or something or some place or some body, loving them so deeply and fully, can break you, as surely as water slamming through a levee. But like water, you need this fire to survive.

Mermaids can be hard to love because nothing will own their hearts more than the sea. Displaced mermaids, those without their tails, have a hard time loving. That is, they have a hard time surrendering. Loving and surrendering do not mean the same thing, except in certain contexts. Do not confuse them for one another in places they do not overlap.

If you fall in love with a displaced mermaid and it turns sour, know that she will do anything to find her tail, and that her heart never truly belonged to you in the first place.

When I went to New Mexico the first time with my family, and then every subsequent time I traveled west after this, I wanted to touch the desert and absorb the heat from the land into my skin. I was entranced by the way the earth appeared scorched and orange, yet still provided life for so many green things, proof that there must have been water somewhere. This was not how I had imagined the desert, and in its divergence from my expectations, I fell in love.

The awe I felt in the presence of the desert was similar to what I felt on another family trip we had taken to Lake Superior, the relief that flooded me as we were greeted with the wide expanse of water after hours of driving through tightly packed crops of trees—the openness of Lake Superior (similar, perhaps, to the openness of Crater Lake, where my grandpa worked as a park ranger for five summers) gave my soul the space it needed to stretch out.

In the tiny town of Chimayo, New Mexico, we found *El Sancturio de Chimayo,* a chapel that attracts nearly 300,000 visitors every year as a site of pilgrimage, although for my parents and I it was just a stop on our drive. When we entered Chimayo that first time, gusts of wind made the leaves that had fallen on the ground swirl and the trees tremble. The sky was dark, but not purple. It was the perfect setting of something momentous, all the details exact and deliberate and shining: When we entered the church, we did so through the wrong door, and made our way through a side hallway where offerings were made—the site of discarded crutches and casts, the site of eyes falling on me, causing me to wonder if people thought I was there for a miracle.

I didn't know why I was there, but I had my dad fill a water bottle from the creek that ran behind the church, a creek that was said to evoke miracles, and later, as she helped me take a shower, I had my mom pour the water over my legs. Present me scoffs at this—not the miracle part, but the part in which I equated being able to walk with said miracle. The miracle, of course, is that I stayed sitting down. And so while it may have seemed to the many mystics and believers who would give me a healing blessing that their prayers didn't work, they did, they did, they did.

DREAM

The Creation

You have a dream one night that you—crouching, naked, like a feral animal—are in the corner of a room that's been painted bright yellow. You are a manifestation of repressed emotion, except there is no locked door caging you in, or at least it would seem. You are being hunted for your pelt—that which you have grown to protect yourself from the sharpened knives of those around you, *your own skin deflecting metal*—and people are closing in around the edges of your mind and the edges of your dream. As you open your mouth to snarl, you realize you have fangs. You have become what they have made you, yet it's not what they intended. You are words and human and animal and everything in between.

You have a dream one night that you are three feet away from your favorite writer, a woman whose words leave you woozy and whose presence (apparently) leaves you without language. You are holding a plate of food, it's a reception maybe, a celebration, but the colors are muted and My God you can walk, no wheelchair here, no swimming through water like you normally do through dreams, and *don't you see?* you want to say to this woman. *Don't you see this perfect body, under your spell?* You bite through a strawberry (except strawberry is too predictable, it's the sex fruit, for god's sake), and suddenly her eyes have snapped to yours and she's coming over, long dark hair cloaking her shoulders, and you swallow the strawberry that is not really a strawberry and see flames licking around her tight dress (because writers do have a flair for drama). Replace reception with torture chamber, a pool of water you are laying in and a wire with an electric charge coursing through it. *I know you can do it*, the writer purrs, but of course you *can't*, not even to please her, who really just wants to erase you by devouring you, cells obliterated, but you won't do it, you say no. Suddenly there is yelling and crying and a smashed ink bottle, black everywhere, stories shattered. Your skin hurts to touch.

You have a dream one night—or is it a dream?—that your leg is aching, bone deep, throbbing pain—it's after the fall, in the deep heat of summer and your skin is coated in a sweat that feels post-sex but is actually post-bodily trauma. You are thinking you should cut the offending leg off, and then you are in a sawdust-filled room which smells like rotting peaches and there are the two strongmen straight out of a sideshow and one of them has a chainsaw. Have you ever heard a chainsaw in your dreams? An amputated limb is TOO EASILY a metaphor for things ripped from us, do you understand? This is NOT A METAPHOR.

MERMAID CODA

The Sixth Mermaid

Straddling the line between one category and another is exhausting. Take foam, for example. It's both water and air while simultaneously being neither. It's brilliant and perplexing and, to be completely honest, a little scary. When I look at foam, I can't help but see myself.

In old stories, when mermaids die, we turn into sea foam. That's fitting, isn't it? Neither one nor the other, neither here nor there. There's this one story though, where a mermaid falls in love with a human man and is promised an immortal soul if she marries him. This makes absolutely no sense, least of all because the very definition of humanity lies in its mortality. But I didn't write the story, I'm just here reporting the facts. That glaring inaccuracy isn't my fault.

But get this—in that same story, the human man doesn't marry her, and when she dies, she doesn't turn into seafoam, she *turns into air*. This detail keeps me up at night, when I let it. I lay under the moon, held by the sea, and am consumed by a spiral of thoughts. Does air have a longer shelf life than seafoam? What does that even mean? Is it easier to survive (in life and past death, understand) as something which does not exist between categories? Well obviously. Except, except, except.

I took in all sorts of girls following the king's proclamation. Did I say girls? I meant mermaids. Well, mermaids and girls aren't actually that different. This is what the king knew and what terrified him.

What he didn't realize, and what should have frightened him more than the single mermaid operating individually, is that by publicly announcing our identity as monsters, he was creating a story for us to rally around as a community. Of *course* the individual is separate from the collective. That is, except when it isn't. And another important note: Some mermaids will tell you the siren story isn't true, that we don't actively seek to destroy human males. This, I'm sorry to say, is not the case.

The mermaids that came to this island had a bloodthirstiness in their veins that demanded sacrifice. How could they not? They had been villainized, ostracized, and driven out of their homes by a city of bystanders. I was not there to judge or comment on their anger; I felt it myself, although I had never lived in the city and so had never been subject to the types of horrors these mermaids brought with them. They came to think of me as a sort of Admiral Nelson type; they even fashioned me a sword from an abalone shell to hang at my waist, and demanded I give rousing speeches before hunts. I know they wanted a figure of steel-sharp strength, so that is what I gave them. I'd never combed my hair with a pearl-studded brush (and have yet to meet a mermaid who does), but now I intentionally let my hair turn into a dark, ratted nest. I sharpened my nails into claws. I coaxed crabs and mollusks to shelter in my hair and then emerge during my speeches, crawling over my shoulders and down my sides.

"You are safe here," I'd always tell them. "But no one is going to avenge our sisters for us." These speeches would always happen around a giant bonfire on the sand: a symbol, I suppose, for seemingly contrasting elements—fire and water—existing side by side.

The key to our survival, I eventually realized, was encouraging the displaced mermaids to divorce themselves from the creature they were before: the city-dweller, the friend of humans, perhaps—for some of them—the human themselves. This was both metaphorical and not: there was no going back for the mermaids that made it to this island.

I remember one mermaid the island took in who was particularly distraught at her separation from humanity. When she first got to the island, she lay haggard on the shore, the sea lapping at her tail as if trying to entice her back in. She must have felt the sand shift as I approached, because she lifted her face, hair streaming, and our eyes met. "They have broken me," she said. Her eyes were full, but didn't spill over until the moon rose. From then on, each night, her tears were unending. So much so that the ocean level rose due to the mixing of her salt water with its salt water.

"You have to let them go," I finally told her one night, meaning the unnamed humans she had loved. "You have to let go of the anger and hurt and, yes, infatuation unless you want to continue to wake up each morning with your stomach burning. You have to forget them."

At this point she had stopped crying, perhaps completely drained of her tears. She would learn soon enough that mermaids have the ocean at their disposal and thus can never truly run out of saltwater to cry. But she didn't know this yet, and so she just sat there on the sand, looking exhausted and absent from her body. The flames from the bonfire reflected onto the wetness of her tail and danced there, among her scales. She had thus far refused to join in the hunts, which was fine with me. But the ocean levels were already rising, and besides, the sight of her broken heart caused my own to ache. As aloof as I appeared to those around me, I had come to love the mermaids who migrated to my island dearly. It took a community of others like me to realize how lonely I had been, before.

"I can't do that," the mermaid in front of me finally said. "I need an in between—surely there is an in between?"

There was no in between.

Months spiraled by. She still refused to take part in the hunts and would instead spend her nights uttering "strange wailing cries at the moon." Her lungs never got the hang of working in tandem with her gills, and one day we had to pull her out of the water as best we could, our own tails fighting for traction in the sand. When we eventually laid her on the shore, I turned away from the others to hide my sob.

"Don't—tell—them about—me," she managed to get out in gurgly fits and spurts. That is, her last dying wish was to never be confined to the page.

Author's Note

At the time of writing this, I've been living in my own apartment with the help of around-the-clock caregivers for two and a half years. This was made possible through a Medicaid waiver Exception to Policy which was written by my amazing case manager. It's important to me that anyone reading this knows living on your own as someone who relies on extensive care *is* possible, as difficult as it was for me to put in place.

Still, I rely on the help of others to cover and coordinate my care. Mercury and I take frequent trips home to my parent's house when I'm worn out and need a break from the constant, changing personalities of all my different helpers. My mom comes to my apartment to cover when there's a last-minute hole in the schedule. She also makes necessary care-related phone calls when there's too much on my plate. Friends provide emotional support and physical care when they're in town for the weekend. My care situation is complex and interwoven with every aspect of my reality, much like an underground network of tree roots and other life.

I know how lucky I am to have access to this type of care. And also, I have no idea what the future of my care network looks like. My constant prayer is for a stable and healthy care situation.

We all need other people, human and non-human alike. When we're given no map to follow, we have no other choice but to create our own. Build something beautiful.

Acknowledgements

Writing *Dreams* was a project supported and facilitated by an endless number of people—if I forgot to include your name, please know I am still filled with appreciation for your role in bringing this book to life.

The biggest swell of gratitude to every person who shared time, memories, and words with me for the sake of this book: my parents, grandparents, friends, helpers.

To professors and peers at the University of Kansas who helped shape my MFA thesis which would eventually become this book, in particular: Korbin Jones, L. Favicchia, Megan Kaminski, Marta Caminero, Laura Moriarty, and Sheri Tucker.

To Rebekah Taussig, friend and fellow disabled writer, I'm ever indebted to the map which drew our paths converging in Kansas. I still can't quite believe we get to create magic together. Thank you for your support, words, and authenticity.

To Fi Collins, who read early drafts of essays and embarked on writing projects with me: Ireland was a literal trip. I'm glad we were on it, together.

Charlee Huffman, thank you for your friendship, wisdom, and sharing of Kaw culture. I will forever be grateful for the beauty of Crip space in bringing us together for the first time.

Cyrus Dunham, thank you for believing in this book and telling me to write a preface. Your time and energy reviewing *Dreams* was generous and appreciated, as was your tolerance of Mercury photos.

To Mariah Stovall, thank you for taking a chance on *Dreams* and its stubborn tendency to slip out of categories. You're an amazing agent, phenomenal writer, and genuinely cool person. Thank you for being in my corner.

To Piper Gourley, Rebeccah Sanhueza, and the entire team at Red Hen Press, thank you for giving *Dreams* a home and ushering it into the world in its best form.

Again, to my family, thank you for being who you are. I think we're a bit like those trees in the Hoh, leaning into each other among the moss and stones, creating a magical ecosystem. How lucky I am, to be a part of this forest.

And to Caroline, of course. Thank you for continuing to speak.

I first came across the quote which begins with "The body is not bounded by the skin" and opens this book in Akemi Nishida's article, "Relating through differences: disability, affective relationality, and the U.S. public healthcare assemblage." This quote is pulled from Lisa Blackman's 2010 paper, "Embodying Affect: Voice-hearing, Telepathy, Suggestion and Modelling the Non-conscious," published in the journal *Body & Society*. *The Fifty-Minute Mermaid* is a collection of poetry by Nuala Ní Dhomhnaill written in Irish and translated into English by Paul Muldoon. It imagines a population of mermaids as creatures from pre-Famine Ireland, displaced in a new world that makes no sense to them, haunted by unexpressed memories and fears passed down from generation to generation. The mermaid poems throughout *Dreams in Which I'm Almost Human* (along with "Mo Mháistir Dorcha/My Dark Master") appear in *The Fifty-Minute Mermaid*. Some also appear in *The Wake Forest Book of Irish Women's Poetry*, which is where I first encountered them. "Really, they came from nowhere," Nuala Ní Dhomhnaill once told me when I asked where her mermaids came from.

The second paragraph of "This is a Truth" appeared in an

earlier form as "13 Things, Iowa City," in *Peach Mag.* This piece was inspired by Lily Hoang's "13 Remotely Related to South Bend, Indiana."

The family history recounted in "No Other Choice" came to me through conversations with my parents. I hope that this book does justice to all our beautifully interconnected lives. The incident of ADAPT protesters being removed from their wheelchairs in the US Capitol building was covered by many national news outlets, including *The Washington Post*, which also ran a video. The statistic of people who have undergone spinal fusion surgery later developing PTSD mentioned is pulled from a 2012 study by doctors Kate Deisseroth and Robert A. Hart published in *Spine*: "Symptoms of Post-traumatic Stress Following Elective Lumbar Spinal Arthrodesis."

An earlier version of "Hard Shells" was originally published in *Entropy*.

An earlier version of "Displacement" was originally published in *Mikrokosmos Journal*. "Displacement" uses quotes from three mermaid poems by Irish poet Nuala Ni Dhomhnaill, "An Mhurúch san Ospidéal/The Mermaid in the Hospital," "An Mhurúch Seo 'gainne fó Thoinn Arís/Our Mermaid Goes Under Again," and "Cuimhne an Uisce/A Recovered Memory of Water." The research cited was published in August 2020 by disabilityaction.org, under the title "The impact of COVID-19 on disabled people in Northern Ireland," a report written by Sean Fitzsimons, Dr. Emma O'Neill, and Dr. Alison Crawford.

"Notes From a Class on Trauma" includes quotes and theory pulled from *The Cancer Journals* by Audre Lorde, *The Body in Pain: The Making and Unmaking of the World* by Elaine Scarry, *Cultural Trauma and Collective Identity* by Jeffrey C. Alexander, et al., "Unclaimed Experience: Trauma and the Possibility of History" by Cathy Caruth, *Exile and Pride: Disability, Queerness, and Liberation* by Eli Clare, "Stolen Bodies, Reclaimed Bodies: Disability and Queerness" by Eli Clare, *Testimony: Crises of Witnessing in Literature,*

Psychoanalysis, and History by Shoshana Felman and Dori Laub, "Un/Safe Disclosures: Scenes of Disability and Trauma" by Alison Kafer, "Intersections of Disability Studies and Critical Trauma Studies: A Provocation" by Daniel Morrison and Monica Casper, and "Identification and Difference: Structures of Privilege in Cultural Criticism" by Judith Roof and Robyn Wiegman. "Notes From a Class on Trauma" first appeared in a slightly different form in *APIARY Magazine.*

The study mentioned in "Bruise as Signifier" was published in "Posttraumatic Stress Disorder in Patients After Severe COVID-19 Infection" by doctors Delfina Janiri, Angelo Carfi, and Georgio D. Koztalidis for JAMA Psychiatry. "Bruise as Signifier" first appeared in my chapbook *For When the Shapes Keep Changing,* published by Neon Hemlock Press.

The title of "Hunger" is inspired by Roxane Gay's memoir of the same name. The quote from Rosemarie Garland-Thomson comes from her book, *Extraordinary Bodies: Figuring Physical Disability in American Culture and Literature.* The discussion of tattoos was inspired by Roxane Gay's writing, along with Melissa Febos's, particularly "Leave Marks." The line "palms touching palms" is a nod to the scene in Romeo and Juliet where the two first meet. The line "Hunger leaving me empty" is a very loose nod to the Brandi Carlile lyric "Hunger drivin' you mad" from her song "Throwing Good After Bad." Questions of when it is time to stay and when it is time to leave are inspired by Jenny Boully's work, particularly the essays "Between Cassiopeia and Perseus" and "The *future imagined,* the *past imagined*" from her book *Betwixt-and-Between,* which takes its title from J.M. Barrie's *Peter Pan*. The line "Why is it then that I have feet and yet still refuse to flee?" is taken from Boully's "Between Cassiopeia and Perseus."

Alison Kafer's work referenced and quoted in "The Way the Clock Bends to Our Bodies" is from her book *Feminist, Queer, Crip.* The discussion of the Kaw language came from a conversation I had with my friend and Kaw Nation citizen Charlee Huffman. The quote from Keah Brown is from her February 13, 2021 Tweet.

The majority of the information in "I Don't Know the Difference Between Beginnings and Endings" came from interviews I conducted with my grandparents, whose stories, strength, and love I am forever grateful for. The statistic of 94 percent of COVID-19 deaths occurring in those with pre-existing conditions is taken from the CDC's COVID-19 Death Data and Resources Page. This statistic has been contested (including by our 45th president) and then fact checked and verified by various news sources including Reuters. The research from Atul Gawande is from his book *Being Mortal*. The quote from Anna Tsing is from her book *The Mushroom at the End of the World* (also mentioned in "The Nature of Her Leaving"). This piece also includes a line from Jenny Boully's essay "On Beginnings and Endings" from her book *Betwixt-and-Between*.

An earlier version of "Skeletons" first appeared in *Hot Metal Bridge*. Nuala Ní Dhomhnaill's poem "Mo Mháistir Dorcha/ My Dark Master" was translated by into English Paul Muldoon.

The statistics on abuse of disabled individuals cited in "The Nature of Her Leaving" (and earlier in "In Between the Staying and the Going") is based upon the research of Dick Sobsey and other scholars. Studies have continued to show that people with disabilities are at much higher risk of abuse than their non disabled counterparts, and that the abuse is likely to last longer and be more severe. DisabilityJustice.org is a good place to start for gathering information on this and what can be done to stop it. The discussion of what type of world my friend's child will be born into in "The Nature of Her Leaving" is inspired by Rebekah Taussig's piece in *Time* magazine, "Living in a Tangle of Joy and Pain During the Pandemic" published January 5, 2021. I also quote Akemi Nishida's article, "Relating through differences: disability, affective relationality, and the U.S. public healthcare assemblage," published January 24, 2017, and Leah

Lakshmi Piepzna-Samarasinha's book, *Care Work: Dreaming Disability Justice,* published in 2018. The term "crip magic" is used widely by disability culture activist and performance artist Petra Kuppers. I became acquainted with this term and concept during a writing workshop held by Petra Kuppers, who, along with poet and dancer Stephanie Heit, runs disability creativity collective Turtle Disco. "Crip magic" is also used by disabled artist and activist Syrus Marcus Ware. "The Nature of Her Leaving" and "In Between the Staying and Going" first appeared in my chapbook *For When the Shapes Keep Changing,* from Neon Hemlock Press.

"Six Ways in Which the Body Becomes Narrative" draws heavily on the work of Susan Wendell, Porochista Khakpour, and Rebecca Wanzo. Lines from "The Body as Political Currency" were first published in a blog post on marginalized bodies and the COVID-19 pandemic for Lawrence Talks. The piece I wrote for the *Disability Visibility Project* about the coverage of Jerika Bolen was published in 2016 under the title "Ableism in Journalism: How the Coverage of Jerika Bolen's Story Negatively Affects All Readers." The *Disability Visibility Project* was started in 2014 by the inimitable Alice Wong, whose work I am forever grateful for. The idea of Ugly Laws, 2021, as talked about in "The Body as Disposable" was inspired by Karl Knights's poem on the original Ugly Laws, which mentions Art Honeyman. The quote from the waitress, and all details of this encounter, are taken from Richard Pimental's Opening Plenary for ALDAcon 2018. The number of forced sterilizations in the United States from 1907 to 1963 (64,000 people) can be found in papers on the history of eugenics in our country. The article from *The Salt Lake Tribune* quoted in "The Body as Disposable" appeared on October 25, 2020, and was written by Erin Alberty and Sean P. Means ("Utah's hospitals prepare to ration care as a record number of coronavirus patients flood their ICUs"). The statistic of 42 percent of COVID deaths in Iowa being residents of long-term care facilities is pulled from an article written for

Iowa Capital Dispatch by Clark Kauffman and was published on January 26, 2021 ("More than 40 percent of Iowa Veterans Home workers are refusing COVID-19 vaccine"). Quotes from Naomi Ortiz are from her book *Sustaining Spirit: Self-Care for Social Justice.* An earlier version of "The Body as Disposable" appeared in *Breath and Shadow.* The effort to move Student Disability Services at the University of Iowa to a more accessible location, as mentioned in "The Body as Repressed Emotion / The Body as Volcano / The Body as a Drain on the System," was championed by Kaydee Ecker and Andrea Courtney, both former presidents of UI Students for Disability Advocacy & Awareness (UISDAA).

The NPR piece my mom references in "The Woman Speaks" is from January 26, 2022, by Lesley McClurg ("There's one population that gets overlooked by an 'everyone will get COVID' mentality"). It discusses, among other individuals, the Miller family and their two boys with MEPAN syndrome, Carson and Chase. I reference and quote "You Are Not Entitled To Our Deaths: COVID, Abled Supremacy & Interdependence," an article by Mia Mingus which first appeared January 16, 2022, on her blog *Leaving Evidence.* The #MeToo piece referenced appeared April 4, 2018, on *Rooted in Rights* and was titled "I Needed My Caregiver to Keep Me Alive. She Exploited That Power." Deep gratitude for their permission to use this excerpt. The podcast mentioned in my letter to a composite friend is the "Dendrology (TREES)" episode of Ologies with Alie Ward. The dendrologist interviewed (who has the tree stump and "Unless" tattooed on his arm) is J. Casey Clapp.

"The Water Essay" includes a line from "And Soul," a poem by Eavan Boland.

The six different voices which speak in "Mermaid Interludes" were inspired by a short story in Jeanette Winterson's *Sexing the Cherry,* "The Story of Twelve Princesses." Like the heartbroken mermaid referenced in "Mermaid Coda: The Sixth Mermaid," the twelfth princess eludes capture. The mermaids in these interludes use the line "so many other deaths abounded," which is a reworking of Jenny Boully's "And so many other deaths abound," taken from her essay "Betwixt-and-Between" about Peter Pan, from her book of the same name. She also says in this essay that "In Neverland, death can be performed, but is also very real," a line that is also reworked and integrated into the interludes. The heartbroken mermaid in the Coda "utters strange wailing cries" at the moon, which are words taken from J. M. Barrie's *Peter Pan.* Admiral Nelson, as mentioned in the Coda, was a real person, but is also characterized in Angela Carter's *Nights at the Circus* as the leader and owner of a brothel that happens to house and employ various magical and mythical women. The mermaid's meditation on foam was inspired by Eileen Myles's Foam speech. Mermaids turning into seafoam when dying is mentioned in the original version of *The Little Mermaid* by Hans Christian Andersen, and the original Little Mermaid does turn into air when she dies.

There are countless texts written by disabled and chronically ill individuals that have shaped my understanding of my identity and the art that has come out of it, too many to name here. Still, a smattering of texts that influenced me: all work by Eli Clare, Sins Invalid and the writing they have put out, *The Rejected Body: Feminist Philosophical Reflections on Disability* by Susan Wendell, *Bodyminds Reimagined: (Dis)ability, Race, and Gender in Black Women's Speculative Fiction* by Sami Schalk, *The Right Way to Be Crippled and Naked,* edited by Sheila Black and Michael Northern, *Beauty is a Verb: The New Poetry of Disability,* edited by Sheila Black and Michael Northern, *The Pretty One: On Life, Pop Culture, Disability, and Other Reasons to Fall in Love with Me* by Keah Brown, *Sitting Pretty: The View from My Ordinary Resilient Disabled Body* by Rebekah Taussig, *Autobiography of a Face* by Lucy Grealy, *Sustaining Spirit: Self-Care for Social Justice* by Naomi Ortiz, *Disability Visibility: First-Person Stories from the Twenty-First Century,* edited by Alice Wong.

Biographical Note

Hannah Soyer is a queer disabled writer living in the Midwest. She has written for nationally acclaimed publications such as *The Sun Magazine*, *Bustle*, and *Cosmopolitan* and is the editor of *The Ending Hasn't Happened Yet: An Anthology of Disability Poetics* from Sable Books (2022). Her chapbook, *For When the Shapes Keep Changing*, won the 2021 Nonfiction OutWrite Chapbook Competition. Hannah also happens to be a cat and chocolate enthusiast.